FRAGMENTED MEMORIES
of A
Man Child

SURVIVING THE PERPLEXITIES
OF TRAUMA AND ADDICTION

DONALD M. SMITH MSW, LMSW

Published by:
Fortune Publishing Group
E-mail: info@fortunepublishinggroup.com
www.FortunePublishingGroup.com
Phone: (888) 910-6370

ISBN 13 : 978-1-955358-37-8
Printed in the United States of America
Book Cover designed by Max Fortune

Table of Contents

Chapter 1: It takes a Village — 1
Chapter 2: The Veney Brothers — 11
Chapter 3: The Tyrant Stepmother — 17
Chapter 4: New Discoveries — 21
Chapter 5: The Birth of Trauma — 27
Chapter 6: Cherished Memories — 31
Chapter 7: Welcome Home — 35
Chapter 8: Moving On Up — 41
Chapter 9: Lost in Trauma — 47
Chapter 10: The Abyss of Addiction — 55
Chapter 11: Jeopardizing Life — 59
Chapter 12: Tragedy Strikes Again — 63
Chapter 13: Pennslyvania Avenue: A Whole New World — 67
Chapter 14: A Tragic Event — 73
Chapter 15: An Evening Excursion — 77
Chapter 16: Hagerstown: An East Baltimore Reunion — 81
Chapter 17: Mind Games — 87
Chapter 18: The Bank Withdrawal — 93
Chapter 19: The Second Time Around — 99
Chapter 20: Prison Paradise — 103
Chapter 21: Karma Makes a Visit — 109
Chapter 22: Revengeful Sex — 119
Chapter 23: A Temporary Release — 129
Chapter 24: Sick and Tired of Being Sick and Tired — 135
Chapter 25: A New Beginning — 141

Chapter 26: Self-Discoveries   147
Chapter 27: A Celebration of Life   153
Chapter 28: My First Anniversary   157
Chapter 29: Divine Intervention   163
Chapter 30: Power of Examples   169
Chapter 31: Establishing A Career   173
Chapter 32: A Message from The Universe   177
Chapter 33: On the Prowl   183
Chapter 34: Out of Control   189
Chapter 35: Tragedies In the Workplace   193
Chapter 36: Crossing Racial Lines   197
Chapter 37: Regressed Behaviors   201
Chapter 38: Black Beauty   205
Chapter 39: The Tentacles of Addiction   209
Chapter 40: Positive Influence   215
Chapter 41: Family Dynamics   221
Chapter 42: Two wounded Souls   227
Chapter 43: My Children   233
Chapter 44: Significate Losses: 245
            The Generational Curse
Chapter 45: The Lessons of Death   253
About the Author   255

Introduction

The contents of this book are my experiences with childhood trauma and years of being addicted to drugs, the street life, and women. My inability to understand and deal with those things complicated my life immensely. Leading me down a road that countless others have also traveled, and some are still on. The sole purpose of sharing my experience, strengths, and hopes is to help others to come to the realization that there is a way out of the perplexities of trauma and drug addiction.

I believe that the first time I used heroin at the age of 16, it was at that very moment when I became stuck in that developmental stage. Although I was developing physiological into a grown man, mentally I remained immature and the traumatized child within me controlled my life and obscured my reality. I could never accept reality as truth, especially when it wasn't benefiting me in some way.

I have come to understand that I was searching for outside solutions to heal inner pain is only temporary reprieve and keeps you stuck in a perpetual state of merely existing with no real understanding what life is about. I also write to give homage to Narcotics Anonymous and those who helped me on this journey towards a deeper understanding of myself.

Witnessing the extraordinary power of one addict helping another instilled in me the understanding that change comes from within.

I inspire to be a living example to those who trauma is continuously running their lives and haven't found their way out of the grips of active addiction. I hope to inevitably give them the option to choose that there may be a more joyful way to live.

Although I have done a tremendous amount of work myself, I am not under the illusion that I have arrived at a place of perfection. My journey of self-discovery will continue until the end of my days.

CHAPTER ONE
It Takes a Village

As I journey through the corridors of my mind, vivid memories of my childhood—memories of joy, pain, and trauma—come flooding back. On November 24, 1955, I was born at Baltimore City Hospital to a single Black woman named Helen Smith. I had seven siblings, and we lived in a small three-bedroom house. I still remember the address: 1919 N. Castle Street in East Baltimore. Although my family had lived in other parts of Baltimore before, moving to Castle Street felt truly magical. We were a typical Black family living in a poor urban area, surrounded by other minority families. Even though we were poor, I have clear memories of a happy childhood, aside from a few terrible events.

We received public assistance, like most families in our neighborhood. Back then, the government did not give out food stamps or food cards. Instead, they sent large boxes of food every month. These boxes contained dry beans, cans of Spam, a thick block of yellow cheese, rice, powdered milk, powdered eggs, and many other items. It was almost magical how our mother could turn these simple, sometimes unhealthy, foods into meals that tasted like they came from a fine restaurant. It also showed how creative and resourceful

Black families could be when it came to survival. I did not realize we were poor until later because every time I flipped the light switch, the lights came on; whenever I was hungry, there was always food to eat; and we were never evicted. I thought it was normal to put cardboard in the bottom of my shoes to cover up holes in the soles. It was just another way we got by.

As a child, I did not fully understand the sacrifices my mother made to give us the best life she could. She took us on trips to Gwynn Oak Amusement Park, where we would spread out our food on old wooden picnic tables. She also took us to Sandy Point Beach, where we swam and enjoyed each other's company.

I remember going to Carr's Beach as a child and watching Bobby Womack perform. Carr's Beach was very popular and was set aside just for Black folks during the time of Jim Crow laws in the segregation era. It gave Black people a break from the constant prejudice, discrimination, and anger in our society. The fun at Carr's Beach also gave us a chance to forget about our troubles and the hard work of a 9-to-5 job.

Even though many of the families were strangers, everyone enjoyed the feeling of togetherness. We shared good food, drinks, laughter, dancing to the music of famous artists, and swimming on the coastal beaches of the Chesapeake Bay in Annapolis, Maryland. Legendary singers like James Brown, B.B. King, Wilson Pickett, Otis Redding, Patti LaBelle, Percy Sledge, The Temptations, and many more were booked to entertain our community.

Looking back, my mother wanted to show us more than just our neighborhood. She filled our home with many books about Black history because she knew the public schools never taught us the real stories of our past. Most of the children in our neighborhood went to the same elementary school, Columbus School #99, on the corner of E. North Avenue and Washington Street, just a half block from where we lived.

I remember November 22, 1963—two days before my eighth birthday—when most of the adults at school were frantic over a news bulletin on TV and radio. In the middle of the day, everyone was sent home. I was seven years old, still in second grade, and I was confused about what was happening. When I got home, my mother explained that President John F. Kennedy had been assassinated. I was more excited about the idea of going outside to play than worried about the sad news. Even though I was happy to be out of school that day, I truly loved my school and the friendships with my teachers and classmates. I was heartbroken when I was transferred soon after.

In 1954, the Supreme Court decided in Brown v. Board of Education that racial segregation in public schools was wrong. Still, it wasn't until I was eight years old in third grade that I was suddenly sent to an all-White school called York Wood Elementary. I did not fully understand the ugliness of racism in America, but I could feel it in the hostile way I was treated. Snooty looks and mean attitudes made it clear I was not welcome there. The adults were even worse than the children. Eventually, at the end of fourth grade, I was transferred back to my favorite school, and I was overjoyed.

The fifth and sixth grades were the best times of my school years. In sixth grade, I became the captain of the safety patrol, helping kids cross the street safely. That year, I had a teacher named Mr. Barlow, a Caucasian man who made a big impact on me. He cared deeply about our education and wanted to show us a different way of living. He even paid for class trips out of his own money because the school did not have any funds. I remember one trip when we saw horses for the first time. The family we visited was wealthy, living in a big house with acres of land and horse stables. I believe that house belonged to one of Mr. Barlow's relatives. Mr. Barlow inspired me to believe there was a life beyond the inner city. I still remember that our sixth-grade graduation theme song was "The Impossible Dream" by The Temptations, a song that touched my heart deeply.

By the time I reached seventh grade, all the morals and lessons I had been taught began to fade away, and my life started to change drastically.

Maya Angelou once said, "It takes a village to raise a child," and that was true for the Black families where I grew up. There was trust and friendship among the families in our neighborhood, and any parent could correct a child's misbehavior. Children in those days were taught to respect adults and elders. We were told that children should be seen and not heard. We were not to disrespect grown folks and had to always say "Yes, sir" or "No, ma'am." If we broke these rules, we risked a major ass-whipping. Many believed in the Bible verse (Proverbs 13:24), "Spare the rod, spoil the child." While this was meant to show that discipline was needed for a good upbringing, most parents took it to mean they should beat their children.

In our family, we were whipped with an extension cord. Sometimes, my mother would even wait until we got out of the tub when our skin was wet and more sensitive, so the lashes would hurt more. I believe that back then, adults often took out their personal frustrations on their children. My sister Carolyn suffered a lot; my mother took her anger out on her because of something that had happened with her father. She was punished for her father's wrongdoings, and it was clear that this was child abuse. I felt so sorry for her. My brother Larry, however, seemed to take the beatings without crying. He would just flinch with every lash.

Most of the families in our neighborhood did not have a father, but there were a few with two parents and some really good men at the helm. The women on our block shared a strong bond and helped each other out. I literally grew up around strong, courageous Black women.

I did not understand at the time how important it was for a young Black child—or any child—to have a strong man who showed care and guidance. I realized this later in life when I started to copy the behaviors of the men I saw around me. Many of those men showed what they thought was strength by acting tough on the outside. In reality, their actions hurt themselves, their families, and the whole community. Their mean attitudes toward Black women showed through their violent behaviors and selfishness. Being around such behavior deeply affected me as a child, and I soaked up those wrong ideas like a sponge. Slowly, those false traits formed a belief system based on incorrect ideas. Eventually, I became a copy of what I saw. Sadly, many Black women believed that a good woman should always be subservient to her man, and some even thought that if a man did not beat her, he did not love her. How insane is that? Even though there were exceptions, these behaviors became deeply ingrained in the minds of many Black men and women. For a time, I was confused about why so many Black folks seemed to hurt themselves and their own people.

Donald Smith

I believe that during slavery, those in power created a wicked plan to keep Black people as property so they could become richer. For three centuries or more, Black men and women were forced to believe that they were only good for picking cotton and serving the White race. This idea was put deep into our minds and passed down from one generation to the next. The purpose of these false beliefs was to break up Black families. I think that self-hatred comes from having painful experiences and feelings of inferiority that lead to violence in our families. Black men with these feelings would create a false idea of what a real man is. This wrong information was passed through Black communities and still exists today, and I, too, became a victim of these false beliefs.

I am not making excuses for my actions or the actions of other Black men and women. I am simply sharing my observation to try to understand the root cause of self-hatred in our communities. I know that broken people try to make sense of their reality by seeking validation for their manhood, whether as men or as young boys. Often, that validation comes through control, violence, and the need to dominate others when they cannot control themselves. Black families and people in society often become victims of these behaviors, and our prisons overflow with Black men, women, and young people.

On our block, there were no grassy lawns—only concrete sidewalks. Everyone in the neighborhood helped collect old car tires. We would paint them, fill the middle with dirt, and plant flowers. Every home had these tire planters in front. There were white marble steps in front of the houses, and once a week, everyone grabbed buckets of soapy water, a can of Ajax, and a scrub brush to clean the steps until they shined bright white. Trash on the streets and in the gutters was unheard of. Families took pride in keeping our neighborhood clean. It was a safe place to live, and neighbors even left their doors unlocked during the day and night.

During the summertime, some of us would sit on those marble steps all night—talking, playing, and having fun until the sun came up. Although we were supposed to go inside when the streetlights came on, we would wait until our parents fell asleep and then sneak out again. I suspect they knew we were outside, but they did not worry as long as we stayed in front of the house. We played hide-and-seek, hopscotch, dodgeball, jacks, double Dutch, and many other games. The children in the neighborhood would get together to play football and basketball, go swimming at the Clifton Park pool, and every Christmas, a gang of us—at least fifteen kids—would go skating through different neighborhoods around Baltimore City. Almost everyone got a set of ball-bearing number five skates for Christmas. Our families could not afford wagons and skateboards, but we were very creative and resourceful.

We made our own wagons and skateboards. We would take grocery carts from the local department store called Two Guys, remove the wheels, and use them to build our wagons. There was one White man on our block named Mr. Honey, and everyone in the neighborhood treated him like family. Mr. Honey was a junkman who collected old stuff from all over Baltimore City. His backyard was filled with junk, and he would give us wood so we could build frames for our wagons. He also gave us metal rods to use as axles to attach the wheels at the front and back of our wagons. For our skateboards, we used a two-by-four and took our old skates apart, attaching them to each end of the board.

On Halloween, we made our own costumes. A couple of my friends and I would dress as hobos. We gathered old clothes with holes in them, collected soot from car mufflers parked in the neighborhood, and smeared the soot on our faces to look dirty. We were very careful not to get the soot in our eyes.

We also ventured around Clifton Park, near the reservoir—which no longer exists. We raced around the reservoir to see who could finish first. There was an old, run-down building that looked like an ancient church filled with pigeons, and we would try to catch them. Right off North Avenue and Broadway, there was a very eerie graveyard built in the 1800s. We used to go there, read the tombstones, and collect worms from under toppled stones for a friend's father. He loved fishing and would give us a dime for each worm we caught. Afterward, we would run to Mr. Randy's corner store and buy candy. It was unusual to see a Black man running his own business. Although I had many friends to play with, I also had a wild imagination that allowed me to play alone for hours, and I was perfectly fine. Those were the happiest days of my childhood.

The older teenagers in the neighborhood would have block parties, waistline parties in basements with blue or red lights, and clean-up block parties where everyone looked out for one another. Sometimes, my siblings would have parties at our house. Although I was too young to join in, I would sneak into the basement when it got crowded. I tried to blend in with the crowd, but I was always caught and sent to my bedroom, only to sneak back down and sit on the top of the basement steps, listening to the music and the laughter of the crowd. Occasionally, there were fights with people from other neighborhoods. Fist fights would spill out into the street from disagreements at the parties. People would fight, and the next day, they would be seen hanging out together like they were best friends. My siblings were very protective of one another, and they would fight at the drop of a hat—especially my sister Patricia, who would fight boys, girls, men, or women. It did not matter to her. There were not as many guns in our neighborhood as there are today, but there were a few stabbings. I never heard of anyone being shot, except for one time when a Baltimore City police officer was shot and another was killed by the Veney Brothers.

CHAPTER TWO
The Veney Brothers

There were two brothers known as the Veney Brothers. They became very famous in Baltimore City for committing crimes. The police and the news media even called them a menace to society.

On December 26, 1964, a police sergeant named Jack Lee Cooper was shot to death while the police were searching for the Veney Brothers. Two days before his tragic death, on December 24, 1964, a Christmas Eve liquor store robbery took place, and police lieutenant Joseph T. Maskell was badly hurt.

According to the Baltimore Sun, two men with their faces covered by scarves walked into Lexie's Liquor Store in the 2000 block of Greenmount Avenue on Christmas Eve at about 9:40 P.M. The gunmen ordered the store owner and customers to put their hands on the counter. One of the gunmen noticed a camera above a refrigerator and, as he reached to pull the camera down, his scarf slipped off and revealed a mustache.

Without the gunmen knowing, the store owner pressed a silent alarm to notify the police about the robbery. The robbers made off with close to $2400 as they left the store. As they were trying to make a speedy exit out the front door, to their surprise they were met by Lieutenant Joseph T. Maskell, who was the first officer to arrive at the scene. A struggle started, and Lieutenant Maskell was shot twice by one of the attackers. As he lay on the sidewalk of Greenmount Avenue, his fellow officers came to help him. He was taken to St. Joseph's Hospital where he was in fair condition. One bullet hit his neck and punctured his left lung, and the other hit the upper part of his back and punctured his right lung. In the midst of helping Lieutenant Maskell, the robbers escaped.

Two days later, Sergeant Jack Lee Cooper and two other officers met in the 1600 block of Carwell Street, about eight blocks away from the liquor store robbery. Two of the officers drove along Gorsuch Avenue. They last saw Sergeant Cooper sitting in his patrol car. At about 4:50 A.M., the two officers heard gunshots and rushed to the 1600 block of Cars Street. They found Sergeant Cooper lying on the sidewalk in the 2600 block of Kennedy Avenue, bleeding from three gunshot wounds. He was rushed to Union Memorial Hospital, where he was pronounced dead at 5:05 A.M.

Three empty brass .32-caliber cartridges were found under Sergeant Cooper's body. Two of the shots had entered his chest, and one had pierced his heart. The police also found a card case and a driver's license. Two of the three men suspected in the robbery were identified as Samuel Veney, 25, and his brother Earl Veney, 31. (The Sun (1837–); December 26, 1964; ProQuest Historical Newspaper: The Baltimore Sun pg.36)

The largest manhunt in Baltimore City history was launched to find the two Veney Brothers. Countless police raids were carried out in Black communities. During these raids, the police violated the constitutional rights of many Black families. Not only were their rights taken away, but their dignity and respect were also harmed during the search for the Veney Brothers.

There were many false tips and reports of sightings of the brothers that led the police on wild goose chases. These false reports only frustrated the police and made the search for the brothers even more intense.

The attorneys for the NAACP Legal Defense Fund filed a petition in U.S. federal court asking that the Baltimore City police stop using unlawful tactics to enter and search hundreds of Black families' homes in their hunt for the Veney Brothers. In the end, Chief Judge Clement F. Haynsworth and his four colleagues ruled that there was not enough evidence to support charges of racial profiling or discrimination in the conduct of the police searches. The court also said that the injunction requested by the NAACP attorneys would be hard to write, hard to enforce, and would put a heavy burden on both the police department and the court. (Afro-American (1893); Baltimore, MD, 11 June 1966: pg. 17)

On January 1, 1965, the police carried out four raids at the same time in East Baltimore. One of the homes raided belonged to a family on my block with the last name Veney, but they were not related to the Veney Brothers. (The Sun (1837–); January 2, 1965; ProQuest Historical Newspaper: The Baltimore Sun pg.28) A large group of police, along with a SWAT team, surrounded the home of the Veney family. They used military-style equipment and breached the front door with a large metal battering ram. As they entered the house, I could hear screams coming from inside. The police escorted the family out of their home and made them sit on the curb. After they ransacked the home from the top floor to the basement, they left quickly, leaving everything in disarray, including a broken front door. Everyone in the neighborhood helped the Veney family fix their home.

The event was covered by the three news networks and was on local TV for days. In those days, there were only three channels—NBC, ABC, and CBS. Each channel would sign off at exactly 11 o'clock with a message like, "It's 11 o'clock, do you know where your children are?"

After the incident, most of the Black community was very angry after watching the news and reading the newspapers. Black families began to rally around the Veney Brothers, hoping they would not be caught.

In all, more than 300 doors were bashed down by police, but the Veney Brothers were never found in Baltimore. Later, the police action was described by the 4th U.S. Circuit Court of Appeals in Richmond, Virginia, as "a series of the most flagrant invasions of privacy ever to come under the scrutiny of the federal court."

Not long after the manhunt, the Veney Brothers were found working in a zipper factory in New Jersey. Their trip back to Baltimore by train was memorable because the brothers became the first pair of siblings to make the FBI's Most Wanted List.

In 1966, the Veney Brothers went to trial in Frederick. Samuel Veney was convicted of Sergeant Cooper's murder and received a life sentence. He is still serving his time at the Rockbridge Correctional Facility. Earl Veney was convicted on two counts of armed robbery, one count of assault, and one count of assault with intent to murder. He received a 30-year sentence.

In March 1976, officers at the Maryland House of Correction in Jessup found Earl Veney hanging dead from a rope made from a bedsheet. (Nawrozki, J. The Sun; Baltimore, MD. January 20, 1993: 13A)

Rumor has it that Earl Veney was murdered by prison authorities in retaliation for the killing of Sergeant Jack Lee Cooper of the Baltimore City Police. Little did I know that many years later, I would end up serving time in the same facility as Samuel Veney.

CHAPTER THREE
The Tyrant Stepmother

There was one family with children who never joined in our games or activities. Their father ran his home with an iron fist. People said he even put chains on the refrigerator and kitchen cabinets. When he was away in the community, the children would gather by their basement window to talk quietly, as if they were prisoners, and they were very scared of him. I do not remember ever seeing their real mother. There were five children in all—four girls and one boy. Two of the girls were twins. Their father was a martial arts instructor, and he taught his son those skills too. Later, I found out that this family was distant cousins to my own family; their mother was related to my mother's side.

Growing up in that home must have hurt the children deeply. One of the siblings eventually moved in with us, and she explained what really went on in her house. Her own mother had died when she was only seven years old. Her father, who had little education and very few dollars, could not easily take care of five children. Child Protective Services soon became involved, warning that they might take the children away if their father could not prove he had a plan to keep them safe and fed. Desperate for a solution, her father made an arrangement with an eighteen-year-old woman to marry him, hoping that having two parents would satisfy Child Protective Services. Once the children seemed safe in a two-parent home, CPS stopped their visits.

But their father was a womanizer. He stayed out all night, leaving his children in the care of his young wife—a young woman who herself was hurt and confused. She had hoped for love and attention from her new husband, but he gave that to other women during his long nights away. Feeling powerless, she took out her anger on the children. She became a tyrant in her own home.

This young stepmother would chain the refrigerator and lock the kitchen cabinets so the children could not get to the food. While their father roamed the streets, she would lock the children in the basement for hours on end. This went on for many years. It soon became clear that the children were not getting enough to eat. Rumors began to spread that they were starving.

In a desperate attempt to silence the gossip, the father and his young wife bought five large cans of spaghetti and five boxes of crackers. They forced the children to eat every last bite. The children ate until they were too full to swallow another mouthful. But just when they thought the meal was over, they were forced to eat ice cream. It came out in such a way that the spaghetti, crackers, and ice cream would burst from their mouths like water from a fire hose.

One of the siblings left home when she was sixteen and never told anyone where she went. The twins eventually got married, and the boy and the other girl also left on their own. In time, the cruel stepmother and her husband separated.

The man stayed on Castle Street for many years by himself. I later heard that he worked at the Great Blacks in Wax Museum, where he helped design wax figures of famous Black people until the day he died.

CHAPTER FOUR
New Discoveries

My mother was a strong Black woman who was very resourceful when it came to taking care of her children. Although I never heard her say, "I love you," I could feel her love in the way she treated and cared for us. I even believe I was her favorite child—I was spoiled rotten. I can honestly say that I never heard her use bad language or see her drink alcohol. I'm sure she might have done those things sometimes, because many of the adults in the neighborhood would hang out at the local bar called the Castle Inn, but I never heard it from her mouth.

My mother taught her seven children to be completely independent. She taught us how to cook, clean, wash clothes, and even iron them. She showed us how to use a sewing machine when we were very young. I can still hear her say, "As soon as your feet hit the floor, make your bed." We all became very good at these things. My brother Marvin even made tuxedos and prom dresses for anyone in the neighborhood who was going to their high school prom, and he charged a small fee for it. She also taught us morals, principles, values, and the importance of education. Every Saturday, our whole house had to be cleaned from top to bottom before we could go outside. We even cleaned the baseboards! While we worked, R&B music played loudly throughout the house, and we would sing, dance, and clean all at once. This is how music became so important to me. I couldn't sleep at night unless I had music playing on the radio in my bedroom. Back then, there were only two Black radio stations in Baltimore City, WWIN and WEBB. My favorite radio DJs were on WWIN—Fat Daddy, Al Jefferson, and Hot Rod. I also learned that the King of Soul, Mr. James Brown, owned the WEBB radio station.

We had a HiFi stereo at home, and I would gather all my mother's vinyl records and play them for hours. I even used a hairbrush as a microphone, standing in front of a mirror and lip-syncing to the songs, pretending to be Smokey Robinson, Marvin Gaye, David Ruffin of The Temptations, and other singers of that time. Over time, I actually became a pretty good singer. When my mother was not home, I would sneak around listening to X-rated comedians like Redd Foxx, Rudy Ray Moore, Moms Mabley, and Pigmeat Markham, and even Bill Cosby, although he never used bad language. Even though I loved music, drawing came second to it.

I spent hours practicing drawing my favorite cartoon characters like Spider-Man, Superman, Batman, The Hulk, Thor, Aquaman, and the X-Men. I was a huge fan of the Marvel heroes. At school, I even competed with a classmate who was very good at drawing from memory. While I was not as strong at drawing purely from memory, if I could see the characters, I could draw them very accurately. Over the years, my drawing skills improved a lot, and they even became a way to earn money for things I needed from the commissary when I was later incarcerated.

I knew little about my mother's upbringing until I met her teenage friend named Loraine, everyone called her Baby-Sis. Now she is 95 years old. Baby-Sis is the sister of my older brothers' father, whose name is Jerome. I also met my brother Clearance's two children. I barely remembered his daughter because she was named after our mother, Helen Smith, and his son, Clearance Jr., looked just like his father. There was also a third son, but no one knew where he was. Baby-Sis and I met at the viewing of my brother Sylvester's girlfriend. Sylvester and Lydia had been together for 28 years. Sadly, she passed away from complications after a gastric bypass surgery. She loved my brother so much and did anything for our family. Her death took her away far too soon

Although it was a sad time, I was very happy to meet Baby-Sis and ask her questions about my mother that I had always been curious about. She told me that she and my mother had been friends since they were teenagers. Baby-Sis was fifteen and my mother was sixteen when they first met. She said that she introduced her brother Jerome to my mother, and the three of them went to Dunbar High School together. They even worked part-time at Johns Hopkins Hospital.

When my mother was seventeen, Jerome impregnated her with her first child, Sylvester. Baby-Sis was there when my mother's water broke. She was just sixteen and did not know what to do, so she waved down a passing taxicab. The taxi driver quickly understood that a teenager was about to have a baby and rushed her to City Hospital. He did not charge a fare because we did not have any money anyway. Baby-Sis smiled broadly when she told me she was the second person to hold baby Sylvester when he was born. Sylvester was raised in his father's family home, where Baby-Sis began to spoil him rotten. My mother and Jerome stayed together for many years and had two more children, Marvin and Larry, who were raised in my mother's home.

Baby-Sis told me that Jerome eventually joined the Armed Services, leaving his childhood sweetheart behind. After that, my mother began a relationship with another man named James Watson. She became pregnant with her fourth child, and my brother Clarence was born. Baby-Sis did not know James Watson personally. I remember her saying that she convinced my mother to tell Jerome she was carrying another man's child, so that he would not come home and find out from someone else. That event ended my mother's long relationship with Jerome.

Before the cheating incident, Jerome was completely devoted to my mother. But after that, he turned into a womanizer. He began having casual relationships with many women. Even though my mother and Jerome were no longer a couple, they sometimes snuck off together. Jerome, whose street name was Bubbles, was always well dressed, a clever hustler, and a ladies' man. Baby-Sis said she did not know exactly what his hustle was, but she knew he was involved in something shady. He became very popular in our neighborhood, and his need to be with other women seemed to be a part of who he was. She said he had children in Baltimore, Philadelphia, and who knows where else.

Even though he did not actively participate in his sons' lives, I remember that he would sometimes show up during family gatherings and special occasions. My mother was an amazing woman, but she often chose the wrong men. She was quite promiscuous, and my sisters Patricia and Carolyn, and I, the youngest boy, all had different fathers. Along with Marvin, Larry, Clarence, Patricia (Pat), Carolyn, and me, our home was full of brothers and sisters, while Sylvester lived with his father's side of the family.

I have come to understand how serious traumatic experiences during childhood can be, and how they affect a person's mind, body, soul, and spirit. Unhealed trauma can lead to terrible outcomes, as seen in the stories of serial killers like Jeffrey Dahmer, Ted Bundy, and John Wayne Gacy. I have heard that trauma can sometimes push a person to succeed, but that was not the case in my family. My mother's habit of choosing abusive men was driven by her own unresolved childhood trauma. What were those painful experiences that made her feel not good enough, not worthy of a loving relationship? She always seemed to find love in all the wrong men.

I do not have any memories of who my father was. There are no pictures or stories about him. There came a time in my life when I desperately wanted to know who my biological father was. I would often ask my older siblings about him, but I always got vague answers. I was once told that he was from North Carolina and came to Baltimore City where he met my mother, and that he died in a car accident on his way back to North Carolina. Maybe they told me that to stop me from asking too many questions—I do not really know what the truth is.

I did not understand how important it was to have a strong, positive Black father to guide me through life. His absence left a hole in my heart that I have tried to fill ever since. Throughout my life, I subconsciously searched for father figures, gravitating toward older men for guidance. My father's absence had a huge impact on me, and it took many years for me to realize that I would never feel whole until that void was filled. Although my older brothers were there to help guide me, they did not have the emotional support that I so desperately needed.

I learned a lot from my mother. She taught me and my siblings to be self-sufficient, but she did not know how to teach boys to become men. So, I searched hard to fill that empty space in my heart by looking up to older men. Unfortunately, I ended up gravitating toward the wrong group of guys for guidance. I saw in them the same qualities that I had seen in the men around me when I was a child. Over time, I became a mirror image of what I saw growing up.

CHAPTER FIVE
The Birth of Trauma

My youngest sister Carolyn's father was named Mr. Carol. He and my mother had a very stormy relationship filled with frequent arguments and physical fights. I can barely remember his face now, but his actions left a deep, painful mark on my soul. I was about nine years old, in fourth grade, and it was summertime—a bright, sunny day when I was not in school. That day, only three of us were home: my mother, Mr. Carol, and me. My mother and a neighbor were sitting on the front steps while I played with my superhero action figures in front of the house. I suspect that Mr. Carol and my mother had a huge argument prior to her coming outside because I overheard my mother and her girlfriend talking about her terminating her relationship with him, somehow I sensed something very bad was about to happen. I never suspected that my mother would become a victim of domestic violence that day.

While I was busy playing, Mr. Carol stuck his head out of a second-floor window and called for my mother to come inside for a minute. I had no idea that he was still in the house. With a heavy heart, my mother agreed and went back inside. About twenty minutes later, I heard her screaming as she ran out of the house. I never heard her scream like that before. I will never forget how I saw her skin and clothing begin to melt away right before my eyes. In that terrifying moment, our neighbor Mrs. Mickey rushed to help. She quickly covered my mother's partially exposed body and called an ambulance.

What we did not know at that time was that Mr. Carol was in the house, mixing a strong, heated solution of lye water—a very dangerous, alkaline liquid. That caustic solution burned my mother's skin so badly that it caused some of her clothes to melt away. Those horrific burns led to many weeks of hospitalization, numerous skin grafts, and permanent damage that she would carry with her forever. My mother wasn't the only one who was permanently scarred that day.

I felt a surge of anger that overwhelmed my small body. I raced toward my mother, not knowing what to do, consumed by a mix of anger and confusion. Mrs. Mickey, who was a nurse, took my mother to the front of her house, and when the ambulance arrived, she went with her to the hospital. In my raging anger, I immediately ran into the house to confront Mr. Carol, but he dashed out the back door. I chased after him, crying and shouting, I was blinded by so much rage that I never thought about what a nine-year-old could do to a grown man. I ran down the alley and even a block away from our house searching for him, but he was nowhere to be found.

Then, suddenly, all that anger was replaced by a paralyzing fear of losing my mother. I raced back home to check on her, only to find that the ambulance had already taken her to Johns Hopkins Hospital. I later learned that Mrs. Mickey worked as a nurse at Johns Hopkins, and her husband was a doctor.

That devastating experience stopped my growth in its tracks and left deep wounds inside me. Even now, there are days when I can see that horrific moment in my mind and feel exactly like that frightened, angry nine-year-old all over again.

When Jerome and my brothers found out about what had happened, they immediately made a plan to find and kill Mr. Carol. They searched all over Baltimore City, but they could not find him. Rumors began to spread that Mr. Carol had moved to an unknown location in New York City, leaving behind a traumatized mother and a shattered family. That terrible event had a ripple effect throughout our family, and each of us began to see the world through our own lens of pain. We all dealt with that trauma in our own unhealthy ways.

During a conversation with Baby-Sis, she spoke about the lye incident, and what she revealed completely stunned me. Apparently, after Mr. Carol had fled to New York, my mother told Baby-Sis that she was still in contact with him. On one occasion, she even traveled to New York to visit him. Her urge to make peace with Mr. Carol overcame her, and she actually forgave the man who had mutilated her and nearly killed her. Even though she shared this painful secret with Baby-Sis, she never told anyone Mr. Carol's exact location in New York because she knew that Jerome and my brothers would go after him. My family never knew about that visit, and I never shared it because I did not want anyone to judge my mother's decision or tarnish her character. Many people do not understand the complicated dynamics of domestic abuse, and neither do I.

CHAPTER SIX
Cherished Memories

During my mother's long stay in the hospital, her friend Mr. George became a constant presence in our lives. He visited her often, and he also helped support our household with money while she was away, making sure there was a safe place for her to come home to. In time, we began to see Mr. George as part of our family—a true blessing during a time filled with deep sadness.

Mr. George wasn't a guy from the streets, he held a steady job. Still, he liked to spend time at a bar called the Castle Inn. The Castle Inn was a lively place with a mix of people, especially on the weekends. There were those who worked hard all week and went there to forget about their troubles, as well as unscrupulous characters always looking to swindle money and possessions. There were loan sharks, street hustlers selling illegal drugs and running numbers, people who always needed a handout, and even some men who were respected because of their money, power, and influence in the community. This mix of characters made the Castle Inn a perfect storm of trouble.

One summer night, while me and some other kids from the were playing our usual games, we saw three guys walking up the street. Two of them were carrying the third, who had a bloody towel wrapped around his neck. As they got closer, I realized that the bleeding man was Mr. George. Even though Mr. George was a solid, hardworking guy, he never backed down from a fight. Apparently, he had gotten into a physical altercation at the Castle Inn. I was told that while Mr. George was beating a guy up, he suddenly pulled out a switchblade and sliced Mr. George on the neck. Thankfully, the two men who carried him home pressed a towel tightly against his wound which kept him from bleeding out and dying. When Mr. George returned from the hospital he had a lot of stitches across his neck. He told us the doctor said the blade had just missed his jugular vein. He was one very lucky man.

After my mother's hospitalization, my sister Carolyn and I went to live with my grandmother, while my other siblings stayed in the household on Castle Street. My grandmother was a small-framed woman with a huge heart—a dignified, elderly Black woman who was the matriarch of our family. I have no clear memories of my grandfather; my grandmother lived alone. Baby-Sis once told me how much she adored my grandmother and mentioned that she remembered my grandmother having a partner named Mr. George. She said that Mr. George had suddenly disappeared, and she never got any details about where he went.

It seemed that not having a father figure was a pattern that spanned generations in our family. My grandmother, like my mother, was a strong Black woman. To this day, I shamefully admit I never learned my grandmother's full name; I only knew her as Mama. She had five children—Luther, Paul, Margaret, my mother Helen, and Raymond. My aunts and uncles are all gone now. Luther died from chronic diabetes, Paul from liver complications, Margaret from cirrhosis due to long-term alcoholism, and I am not sure how Raymond died, but I suspect it was related to alcohol or drugs. My mother, too, eventually passed away from heart failure. The disease of addiction and its sorrowful consequences ran through two generations of my family.

I have many happy memories of living with my grandmother. Like my mother, Mama was a stickler for keeping our home spotless. There was always music playing on the radio. Even now, I can still hear The Marvelettes singing "Please Mr. Postman," The Drifters crooning "Under the Boardwalk," Aretha Franklin belting "Ain't No Way," and Curtis Mayfield & The Impressions singing "Choice of Colors," along with many other all-time great songs. Every Sunday, we gathered around the TV to watch The Ed Sullivan Show, eagerly expecting to see Black entertainers perform. We also watched shows like The Red Skelton, Carol Burnett, and Flip Wilson—laughing with her was one of my favorite memories, especially when Flip Wilson came on because he was so funny. We often went shopping with my grandmother. All the stores were close to her home—we would walk to Goldenberg's, which was like the Family Dollar of our time, and Sears & Roebuck was right across the street. After shopping, she'd take us to Arundel Ice Cream, our favorite ice cream store.

One day, my grandmother took me to visit my mother at the hospital. As I entered her room, vivid images of that horrific day flooded my mind. I was instantly overwhelmed with a flood of emotions. I saw my once beautiful mother, with her face still scarred from the lye incident, and all the feelings inside me exploded like a raging volcano. I began crying hysterically, shouting, "That's not my mother!" and I ran out into the hallway, letting out a gut wrenching cry that seemed to reverberate throughout the hospital walls.

Donald Smith

That day, when I saw the deep scars on my mother's face, I knew I would carry that image in my heart forever. It was a day that changed my life—a day when anger, fear, love, and sorrow mixed together into a memory I cannot erase.

CHAPTER SEVEN
Welcome Home

After several weeks of skin grafts and physical therapy, my mother finally came home. The images of her lying in that hospital bed were ingrained in my mind. So, I was very reluctant to enter the house to see her. I finally mustered up enough courage to go see her. To my surprise, she looked like the mother I remembered before the incident with the exception of some visible burn marks on her neck, arms, chest, and face. The doctors had done a remarkable job with restructuring her appearance. People from the neighborhood came to see her, and I ran towards her and gave her a really tight hug. Her presence made me feel whole again.

We became overly protective of her, and by this time, Mr. George was a permanent household member. Whenever my mother and Mr. George had an argument, we would hang around the house telling each other, "As long as he doesn't touch her, he will be alright, but if he does, he will get the ass whipping of his life."

My mother's traumatic event affected all of us deeply. We were unaware of the pain simmering inside us and how it would slowly change our lives. We didn't have the knowledge or money to seek therapy—and, to be honest, the idea never even crossed our minds. In fact, many in our community didn't believe in therapy; instead, we found comfort in our unwavering faith in God—the same strength that carried our ancestors through the horrors of slavery. So, my family continued on with our lives, carrying the unresolved trauma within our minds, spirits, and souls, and over time, it began to erode the morals and values our mother had taught us.

My brother Marvin was very careful with his things. I remember borrowing his bicycle, and when I returned it, he noticed a small scratch on the fender. He was so angry that he told me I could just keep the bike. The girls in the neighborhood adored his charming personality and his knack for dressing well; he even made most of his own outfits. Eventually, he became the father of three young teenage girls from our block, though not all at once. Ironically, one of these women was named Helen, just like our mother. I sometimes wonder if he chose a woman with our mother's name because of the guilt he felt for not protecting her on that tragic day. Unresolved trauma and pain can shape our thoughts and actions in many ways as we try to cope with our inner emotions.

Although Helen was the mother of his first child, Cynthia became his loyal partner. She would do anything in her power to keep him. Cynthia was one of nine children, and her parents were very religious—one of the few families on our block with two parents in the house. They lived about three doors up from us. I still remember an incident when one of her siblings, who was around eight years old, was playing near the stove and got a pot of hot chicken grease spilled on his head. He was hospitalized, and when he came home, there was a long, noticeable scar where his hair once was.

Cynthia and Marvin had a turbulent relationship. They often had physical and verbal fights, but Cynthia's determination eventually won out. She and Marvin got married and had three children: Marvel, Gregory, and Dana. Gregory, the oldest, was diagnosed with a Level 1 autism spectrum disorder, and both the family and the neighbors were very protective of him. Cynthia and Marvin even bought a house right across the street from our family. Although they were married, my brother never stopped seeing other women, but he was still a good father and provider.

Meanwhile, Helen gradually faded from Marvin's life, yet she continued to live on the block. She was a wholesome woman and a very attentive mother to her son, little Marvin, who eventually joined the service. He later became a Secret Service Agent in Washington, D.C., assigned to protect the Vice President—and we were all so proud of him. The third woman with whom Marvin had a child was named Marylou, though we called her Mary. Her family moved from Frederick, Maryland to Castle Street, where about ten children lived together and spoke with a heavy Southern accent. One of her brothers even married my sister Pat.

My brother Clarence was an introvert and a deep thinker. He didn't mingle with everyone; he was very picky about who he chose to spend time with. As far as I can remember, Clarence always had some kind of side hustle going on. He even fell in love with the next-door neighbor's daughter and started dating her. I don't remember her name, but I do remember that her brother had the nickname "Dump." Years later, Dump became known for robbing drug dealers and others who bought drugs in East Baltimore. Although Clarence and I took very different paths in life, our journeys would cross in later years. Even though Clarence went to school and worked different jobs, there was always something about him that sparked my curiosity. I later learned that he spent his free time selling marijuana. Eventually, he moved on to selling cocaine and heroin, and he became one of the largest, low-key drug dealers in East Baltimore. He was very smart about keeping himself separate from the day-to-day handling of his products. He even recruited my brother Marvin, who put together a group of loyal young men to help distribute the drugs. Marvin worked as a Baltimore City Firefighter. I will discuss later how that lifestyle affected them both and how their unresolved trauma played a significant role in their downfalls.

My brother Larry coped with his trauma and pain through laughter. He had a natural gift for comedy, and I believe he missed his true calling as a standup comedian. Larry was hilarious; people loved being around him because there was never a dull moment. Larry and I even shared a bedroom, and I always saw him as my favorite brother because we played together as kids. We were both very good at sports, playing football, basketball, and baseball with other neighborhood children. We also loved watching WWE and were fans of old-time stars like Bruno Sammartino, Bobo Brazil, Andre the Giant, and Haystacks Calhoun. We didn't know that wrestling was staged—we would put on our swimming trunks, go to our basement, and pretend to be professional wrestlers. Larry especially idolized Bobo Brazil, the only Black wrestler at the time. Sometimes Larry would roughhouse with me until I was nearly in tears. I guess in his own way, he was trying to toughen me up.

In high school, Larry attended Clifton Park High. He had traditional ideas about life—following the law and earning an honest living. Even though he had a righteous side, he also struggled to control his anger. If anyone disrespected him or our family, he would quickly lose his temper. We were all good at fighting—my brothers and even my sister Pat. I remember once seeing Larry charge at a man who had a gun pointed right at him, beating him without mercy. Over time, Larry's unresolved trauma began to change his view of the world, and he became someone I hardly recognized.

I remember one time riding in a car with Larry and some friends. As we drove, Larry saw a dog crossing the street. Without warning, he accelerated and deliberately ran over the dog, killing it. I was shocked and couldn't say a word. The other passengers were stunned too, though they tried to laugh it off and called Larry crazy. I have always believed in karma and the consequences of doing wrong, and I fear Larry would eventually suffer for his actions. In the end, Larry turned to drugs to numb the deep pain inside him.

We called my sister Patricia "Pat" or "Patsy." Growing up without a father shaped the way she dealt with men. The only examples of relationships she knew were the stormy and broken ones our mother had experienced. Pat was feisty and never let anyone push her around, yet she was also very flirtatious. I noticed that, unlike our mother, Pat was a physical fighter. She was determined never to let a man control her, especially after seeing what our mother had endured.

After several meaningless relationships, Pat finally found a good man named Frank. Frank was the brother of Mary, and their family lived in the corner house down the street from us. (Mary was the third woman who became pregnant by my brother Marvin.) Frank and Mary had a son named Jeffery, who later was convicted of murder and spent 30 years in prison.

Pat and Frank had a relationship marked by physical fights—if Pat got a black eye, Frank would too. Even though their relationship was turbulent, they eventually married and had two beautiful daughters, Tonya and Niecy. Their on-again, off-again relationship eventually settled down, but Frank remained a constant in our lives. To this day, he is a great father and always shows up at family gatherings.

Over the years, Pat became the head of her household. Just like our mother, she never felt complete without a man by her side. She always had a bright idea about love that she never quite achieved. Education was not her strong suit, and she eventually dropped out of school. Even though she struggled with reading and writing at times, her survival skills were impressive. Pat didn't take any nonsense from anyone, and she had a kind heart. She also became a foster parent and raised three foster children until they grew up; they truly became part of our family.

My sister Carolyn was treated differently by our mother because of what her father, Mr. Carol, had done. My mother loved and cared for Carolyn, but if she did something wrong, she was harshly punished. Carolyn was the baby girl— sneaky and private about her activities—probably so no bad news would reach our mother. I don't recall seeing her with a boyfriend, but I am sure she had secret relationships. She was very good at keeping her business to herself. Later on, rumors spread that she was involved with a lesbian, but she never confirmed or denied those stories. Although Carolyn never had children of her own, she was great with kids and often babysat for others.

CHAPTER EIGHT
Moving On Up

During the last few months of my sixth-grade year, my family moved to 4230 Ivanhoe Avenue in the Wilson Park area of Northeast Baltimore. I remember my mother giving me detailed instructions on how to catch the MTA bus to my new elementary school. One morning, when I got off the bus in front of the school, I witnessed something that would haunt me for years: three guys were fighting in the street. Two of them were beating up a heavy-set man, and then one of the fighters pulled out a knife and began stabbing him repeatedly. Terrified, I ran into the school building and never mentioned what I had seen.

I graduated from sixth grade and moved on to seventh grade at Woodburn High School. By that time, mischievous behavior was slowly starting to emerge in me, and eventually I was suspended from school. I remember being evaluated by a school therapist because the administrators believed I might have an undiagnosed mental condition due to my uncontrollable behavior. Soon after, I was transferred to Samuel Gompers General Vocational School #298—known as the Gladiator School—located at 1701 East North Avenue, only about three blocks from Castle Street. The school earned its nickname because every Black male who showed troublesome behavior in regular public schools was sent there. The environment was far from conducive to learning; students played dice games on the stairways, fistfights broke out daily, and you could almost buy any drug you could think of. This chaotic atmosphere was new and disorienting for me. I eventually realized that I had a behavior problem, not a learning problem. After about two weeks, I left the school, uncertain of what my next step would be.

My next school adventure was at Hamilton High School, which was entirely Caucasian. The school population was dominated by white kids who openly showed their prejudices toward the few Black students. One day, while I was on my way to class, a white kid deliberately bumped into me and shouted, "Watch where you're going, Nigger!" All I saw was red, and I lashed out. In the middle of the scuffle, a large Black kid named Ricky grabbed me and pulled me away up the stairs to the next floor as school authorities hurried down the hallway. Ricky, who lived just a few blocks away in the Wilson Park area, soon became my friend.

It became dangerous for me to walk through the white neighborhood to catch the MTA bus home. I would pass gangs of white boys on street corners who stared at me and hurled insults. I began to feel that school wasn't a safe place for me, and I couldn't wait until I was old enough to leave it all behind.

The house in Wilson Park was very nice and spacious for our large family. Mr. George moved in with us and continued to be very supportive. The community was pleasant too, with grassy lawns, plenty of trees, and a mix of Black and white families. But that harmony did not last long. Soon, real estate owners started a practice called blockbusting. They persuaded white property owners to sell their houses by warning that Black families were moving in. Once the houses were bought, the owners would rent them to Black families for steady profit. Quickly, the neighborhoods became saturated with Black families.

I was about twelve years old and felt deep grief over leaving my beloved Castle Street—a place that was my utopia. Moving abruptly from Castle Street to an unfamiliar community had a serious effect on me. I was at a crucial stage in my life, trying to form my identity, while all the traumatic experiences from my past were slowly fermenting inside me. In time, the influences around me would shape the person I became.

Across the street from our new home lived a two-parent family with nine children: Marion, Anthony (nicknamed Bubbles), Connie, Angie, Yvonne, Earline, Rodney, Alby, and Michael. Yvonne was the most beautiful girl I had ever seen—a petite, light-skinned girl with lovely brown hair, pretty brown eyes, and a radiant smile. She was always neatly dressed, with her hair usually tied in a ponytail. Even though I had never had a girlfriend before, I felt deep within that she would play a major role in my life, despite not being my first love. I befriended her brother Bubbles and even devised a plan to capture Yvonne's heart.

A girl named Edith, who also lived across the street, was the one with whom I had my first sexual experience. Though I had experimented with other girls at times, I had no idea what I was doing. We would play hide-and-seek, and once I caught one of them, we would act like we were having sex. Neither Edith nor I had ever truly had sex before, and it was very awkward. One night, we snuck into the basement of her house, and we had sex. I could tell she was very nervous because she was trembling. As I began to penetrate her, I worried that I was hurting her when she started to cry. I was too caught up in the intense feeling to stop. Once it was over, I was overwhelmed by the pleasure I had just experienced. Although I sometimes practiced self-pleasure, nothing compared to the explosive feeling of that encounter. I chased that euphoria throughout the rest of my life.

Edith's older sister Linda was dating my brother Larry, and another sister, Jenny, who had some learning difficulties, was also around. Yvonne's brother Bubbles would sneak off with Jenny at night for secret encounters. Every time the guys questioned him about it, he adamantly denied it. Jenny would follow him around, and he would throw things at her to shoo her away, but she would persist, saying, "I love you," over and over, until he could no longer deny sleeping with her. Eventually, Jenny got pregnant and had a baby boy named Jonathan McBride Jr.—which was also Bubbles' birth name.

In time, Edith started seeing someone else, and I began chasing Yvonne. Every time I saw her, I would bask in her beauty. As I got to know her, she started falling for me. Yvonne babysat for people in the neighborhood, and one evening, while she was on duty and the children were asleep, I persuaded her to have sex with me. Our secret encounters continued for a while, and eventually, she became pregnant. On June 9, 1970, she gave birth to my first son, Kevin. I was fourteen years old, and she was sixteen.

When her mother found out, she came over to my house to speak with my mother about the situation. They decided that Yvonne would not have an abortion, and that both families would help provide for the child. Yvonne, once full of hope, became very compliant—almost as if she were available at my beck and call. Once I felt she was mine, I began to explore other options with other girls.

CHAPTER NINE
Lost in Trauma

Trauma has a way of reshaping your morals, principles, and ambitions—even those aimed at achieving success. My mother instilled in me a strong sense of moral standards and honesty, while my sixth-grade teacher, Mr. Barlow, sparked in me a deep desire to succeed through perseverance and hard work. He opened my eyes to a lifestyle beyond the confines of poverty. Meanwhile, Mr. Randy, a Black store owner, revealed the promising possibilities of Black entrepreneurship. Over time, however, my vision of success became distorted, and I ended up unsuccessfully seeking it through criminal means.

My unresolved childhood trauma had an impactful effect on me throughout my life. My growth stagnated at the age of nine the moment I witnessed my mother's horrific event and the discovery of her lifeless body at the age of sixteen. Those tragedies have brought into existence a feckless and gruesome man-child. My mind continuously makes me aware that my inner child is still in the healing process. It evokes vivid feelings and visions of my childhood trauma.

My unresolved childhood trauma impacted me deeply throughout my life. I felt my growth come to a standstill at the age of nine when I witnessed my mother's horrific event, and again at sixteen when I discovered her lifeless body. Those tragedies created within me a feckless, broken man-child. My inner child is still in the process of healing, and my mind constantly brings back vivid feelings and memories of that painful past.

I began hanging out with some of the older guys in my neighborhood and experimenting with alcohol. I started drinking gut-wrenching, cheap wines—Wild Irish Rose, Boone's Farm, Ripple, and Thunderbird—mixed with orange juice. One day, trying to keep up with the older guys, I drunk so much, I felt utterly miserable. I went home to try to sleep off the terrible feeling, but every time I closed my eyes, the room spun around me. I prayed that the horrible sensation would subside, but it simply had to run its course. One might think that after such a bad experience, I would quit drinking. But no—I felt compelled to put on a façade for the older guys, even though deep down, I truly hated drinking.

Bubbles and I became really close friends. His family moved from the Perkins Homes project to Wilson Park. He would take me to his old neighborhood and introduce me to a group of guys that he sung acapella with. I loved music since I was a child imitating my favorite singing groups. Bubbles taught me how to carry notes and harmonize. I became hooked.

He wanted to start his own singing group, so he recruited me and another friend of ours named Jerome. We practiced every day for hours and eventually became really good at it. We attracted large crowds of people listening to us while we practiced our street corner harmony. It was a distraction for me to get away from the activities of the streets, but the lifestyle was beckoning me to return.

Fragmented Memories of a Man Child

We developed a professional sound as our group took shape—Jerome sang tenor, I sang second tenor, and Bubbles held down the baritone. Although Bubbles stuttered when he spoke, his singing flowed with ease. Jerome's voice was so smooth and powerful that he was often compared to Eddie Kendricks of The Temptations. In fact, a talent scout even approached him about joining a new singing group, but Jerome simply replied, "If all of us can't go, then none of us are going."

Around that time, my mother decided we needed a larger house because my sister Pat had just given birth to my niece, Niecy. We moved to 4021 Wilsby Avenue in the same Wilson Park area. Shortly after the move, my mother began working at a laundromat on York Road and Rose Hill Terrace. I would often help her clean the lint traps in the dryers and tidy up the place—I was always very protective of her.

During this period, I was seeing both Jackie and Yvonne, and neither knew about the other until September 27, 1971, when Jackie gave birth to my second son, Dana. I had just turned fifteen, and Jackie, a seventeen-year-old virgin when we met, changed my life in ways I couldn't have imagined. I was slowly becoming someone my family barely recognized, but my mother remained my biggest enabler. No matter what I did, nothing could shake her love and care for me, even though my actions clearly showed signs of self-destruction.

The guys I hung out with were much older than me, so I felt compelled to prove I was tough enough to handle any situation. This mindset made me believe I was invincible, and the praise I received from those older men only inflated my ego further—some even began looking up to me. I earned the nickname "Duck," not after the cartoon character, but

49

because I was always ducking the police or someone I had robbed. I was constantly getting arrested, but as a juvenile, I was always released into the care of my mother or older brothers. The police knew me so well that sometimes I would be taken into custody twice in one week.

I continued to drink alcohol occasionally and started smoking marijuana. I participated in a lot of criminal activities and was finally arrested and sent to a juvenile facility. When most of the adults in the neighbors found out I was arrested, they couldn't believe it, because I had an uncanny ability to project a personality of a well respectable and honest young man in front of older adults. As a young kid, I was taught to respect adults and the elderly, but I could always put on an innocent face leaving them thinking that I was an angel.

I can't quite remember what I was arrested for because I committed so many crimes. I was a fifteen-year-old kid standing in front of a judge. It was probably because of the numerous arrests on my juvenile record. My innocent looks didn't work on the judge. He sentenced me to six months in Boys Village. My mother was present with a look of total disappointment as she started to cry. I wasn't concerned about the six months but seeing my mother crying devastated me. I hung my head down in shame, while the court bailiffs escorted me out of the courtroom.

Boy's Village of Maryland is a juvenile detention center located in Cheltenham, Maryland. Once I arrived, I was sent to an orientational cottage for the first 30 days before entering the general population. I transferred to a regular cottage. After observing the environment and seeing who's the most aggressive kid, I immediately made it known that I wasn't to be messed with. So, I picked a fight with the guy named Barnett who appeared to be the most dominant. At first, I thought I had taken on more than I bargained for because he was getting the best of me, which enraged me. I couldn't allow him to beat me up in front of the other kids, especially after I was the aggressor. I mustered up enough strength to subdue him. Afterwards, we became the best of friends.

I never had the desire to participate in having sex with other guys, but Barnett was bisexual. He had an attraction for a kid that we named Jellyroll. Jellyroll wasn't a homosexual, but he had the shape of a woman, and his ass was plump and slightly jiggled as he walked. If you looked at him from behind, you could easily mistake him for a woman. Barnett was a bully, and he intimidated the kids and Jellyroll was no exception.

One day, Barnett devised a plan to subdue Jellyroll and have sex with him. He requested that I be a lookout to ensure that the staff wouldn't come. The perfect opportunity arrived when Jellyroll was in the shower alone. Barnett went into the shower while I was on the lookout. After the sexual assault, Jellyroll was too afraid to tell staff, and things went on as if nothing had happened.

I noticed that Barnett and Jellyroll would periodically disappear, and curiosity sparked my interest in asking Barnett about their disappearance. He disclosed that they were having sex on a regular basis. Turns out, Jellyroll started enjoying having sexual relations with Barnett. Sometimes, he even initiated the sexual activities.

I remember it was getting close to my sixteenth birthday. Christmas and birthdays were two of my favorite days of the year because my mother gave me the royal treatment.

Giving me whatever my heart desired. Thoughts of leaving Boy's Village were continuously ruminating in my mind. The closer those dates came, the more I thought about leaving. So, Barnett and I devised a plan to AWOL. Both of us were on trash detail for the week, so one night we took the trash out and kept going. It was pitch black and we proceeded across a muddy field towards the highway. With each step our feet would sink into the mud halfway to our knees because it had rained earlier. It was like the muddy field was trying to hold us captive until we were discovered by staff, but our persistence and determination persevered.

It seemed like an eternity but, we finally reached the highway and started hitchhiking. I didn't believe in miracles, but miraculously a Caucasian man stopped and picked us up. Barnett and I looked at each other as if we could read each other's minds. It appeared really suspicious that this white man was picking up two black kids on the highway in the dark of night. If he had a malicious intent to harm us in any way, we were going to beat his ass and take his car. By the way, I had no experience with driving a car and neither did Barnett.

To our surprise, he was very friendly, and he talked about his trip driving to Baltimore. I surmised that he knew that the two of us were escapees from a Juvenile detention facility right across from where he picked us up. He actually dropped us off in downtown Baltimore. Barnett and I went our separate ways because he lived on the Westside, and I lived in Northeast Baltimore. I was completely broke, so I hailed a taxicab, and proceeded to go home knowing that my mother would pay the fare. As I rode down Cator Avenue, an exuberant feeling came over me, I was back in the environment that I called home.

My mother was really surprised to see me and gave me a big hug. She asked if the authorities allowed me to come home for the holidays, I wanted to say yes, but once she looked down and saw my muddy shoes, I couldn't lie. So, I told her that I went AWOL, because I missed her and wanted to be home for the holidays. She said that she would allow me to stay until after Christmas, which was three days away. After convincing her to allow me to stay a week, I immediately changed my muddy clothes and shoes.

I went outside and hooked up with some old friends that freely gave me alcohol and marijuana. After hanging out for a while, and catching up with my homeboys, the first thing came to mind was having sex before I returned to Boys Village. I notified Yvonne and she met me at my house. She was happy to see me and wasn't concerned about the fact that I had escaped from a juvenile detention facility. We spent the entire night having sex and talking about what was going on with family members and people in the neighborhood while I was gone.

My mother always made a big deal about Christmas, and she made sure that everyone had what they wanted. On Christmas day while gifts were being opened, I noticed that there was even something for me. The three days before Christmas, my mother scrambled to ensure that I had something on Christmas day. She was such an amazing woman.

Sure enough, a week after Christmas I was transported back to Boys Village by my mother and my uncle Luther.

CHAPTER TEN
The Abyss of Addiction

After I served the six months in juvenile detention, I returned to my old stomping grounds, and my life took a dramatic turn. Although I was just sixteen, I continued to hang out with older guys and participated in criminal activities. Most of the families residing in the Wilson Park area moved from the roughest parts of East Baltimore trying to establish a new journey from drugs and crime. But most of the drugs and crimes were being committed by the children of those same families. You know what they say, "you can take the child out of the hood, but you can't take the hood out of the child."

Most of the guys were indulging in using heroin or selling it. The persona of heroin addicts in those days weren't like the addicts of today, looking like skeletons in dirty clothes with yellow, rotten, or missing teeth. They were well groomed, neatly dressed, wore silk and wool slacks, alligator shoes, and Kango hats. They were able to look that way because they used real heroin, not a mixture of unknown chemicals that turned people into the walking dead.

The well-groomed guys were one of the attractions that led me to follow their path. Heroin only costs a dollar a pill. We called them buck-pills.

The older guys didn't condone youngsters using heroin, but most of the guys saw me as one of them because I became just as ruthless as them. One afternoon, I was hanging out with an older friend named James. He introduced me to a lot of street games and behaviors, but he was a little reluctant about turning me on to heroin. His reluctance made me even more curious. You know the old saying, "curiosity killed the cat", well eventually, I almost died with him.

After badgering him to turn me on, he finally submitted. He concocted a makeshift syringe out of an eyedropper, placing a rubber band tightly around the black rubber on the end of the eyedropper. He then tore the edge of a dollar bill, rapping it tightly around the tip of the eyedropper and placed a hypodermic needle on it. I watched him as he opened a capsule of heroin and poured the contents into a soda bottle top, added a little water, and he struck a match to heat the bottom of the soda top so the heroin could dissolve. He drew a portion of the heroin into the eye dropper, tied a belt around my arm, and injected heroin into my vein.

The feeling I received was intense euphoria, it took me to a place of nothingness. There were no thoughts of not living up to my family's expectations of being the perfect child. It freed me from the shameful feelings of keeping my mother awake at night worrying about whether she would get a call from the police saying that her son was murdered. I actually became oblivious to all of the neglective thoughts and traumatic events that haunted me throughout my young life. I became this sixteen-year-old kid with two children and caught up in a vicious cycle of addiction.

For the next 23 years, I chased that first euphoric feeling, but I never was able to achieve the same intensity. In a short period, I became addicted to heroin and the lifestyle of the streets. My criminal activities increased to support my drug habit. I became good at burglarizing homes. The neighborhood was still a mixture of white and black families.

One day, I was searching for a house to burglarize, and I unknowingly stumbled upon a police officer's home. By the looks of the inside of the home, he appeared to be a bachelor. He had guns in every room, and I took every last one of them.

Cator Avenue and York Road had become the hangout spots for most of the crew that I was affiliated with. I did the most outrageous things to be accepted because I had an innate need to feel validated, and my antics paid off. We would shoot dice, drink that gut-wrenching Thunderbird with orange juice. Again, I didn't like to drink, so I pretended to drink just as much as they did just to fit in. My drug of choice was heroin. Although I indulged in taking other substances, there was no other mood or mind-altering drug that affected me like heroin. It took me to a place of total oblivion and pacified my weeping inner child.

A friend of mine named Herbie A.K.A Fingers would allow us to use his mother's basement as a shooting gallery as long as something was in it for him. A lot of unlawful activities went on at Cator Avenue and York Road. The entire Wilson Park area and surrounding neighborhoods had become completely occupied by Black families.

One summer night, there was a large number of us gathered at the corner on Cator Avenue and Old York Road. Occasionally guys from other neighborhoods would come to the area to participate in shooting dice or whatever was going on. One of the guys that wasn't form the neighborhood, became upset because he was losing his money, and he accused one of my buddies of cheating. They began fighting and all hell broke loose, everyone jumped on the guy who was the outsider and began beating him badly. People came outside of their houses to see what all the commotion was about.

The disturbance eventually moved in front of my buddy's house. His entire family were friends of mine. They were a household of two parents and five children. Suddenly, multiple shots were fired by one of the outsiders and everyone scattered. A couple of guys grabbed the shooter and held him down. Once things had calmed down, my friend's sister Doreen was lying in the street dead. A bullet had struck her in the head. My friend Michael picked her up and placed her on her family's front lawn. Doreen was also the girlfriend of my singing partner Jerome.

We held the shooter for the police while he was continuously being beaten and kicked on. The police and ambulance arrived. The paramedics tried in vain to resuscitate Doreen, but their efforts were unsuccessful. The paramedics also attended to the multiple injuries of the shooter. Although the shooter was beaten to a pulp, the police handcuffed him and took him to the hospital. He was arrested for first degree murder. That was the first time I saw someone murdered, but unfortunately it wouldn't be the last.

We had received word that the shooter was detained at Baltimore City jail and placed in protective custody. Guys in jail heard through the grapevine what had happened, and several unsuccessful attempts were made on the shooter's life.

CHAPTER ELEVEN
Jeopardizing Life

A drug dealer from New York came into the neighborhood and started selling heroin. Some of his crew I knew, and I gradually became one of the people who tested his product before he sold it. I was there when he cut the heroin with Bonita and Quinine to increase the amount, and to lessen the potency to prevent customers from overdosing. This went on for months until he was found murdered in his car. By this time, I was lost in my addiction. I was willing to do anything whatever it took to obtain money to support my drug habit.

There was a stickup guy named Kenny who was looking for a couple of guys to rob this drug dealer he knew in West Baltimore. He approached me with the proposition, and I gladly accepted. He also recruited another guy from East Baltimore named Brother Mouzone. I don't know if he was a Muslin or not, but what I do know is that he was dangerous and had a collection of weapons stored in his basement. Kenny and I took 9mm handguns and Brother Mouzone had a sawed-off shotgun, and there was a fourth guy who participated as the driver.

Donald Smith

We proceeded to drive to the complex where the drug dealer's stash house was located. Apparently, Kenny knew the guy because when we approached the door, Brother Mouzone and I were on each side of the door, as Kenny knocked. Someone asked who it was and as he looked through the peep hole and recognized Kenny, he opened the door and the three of us bumb-rushed through the door. There were three guys in the apartment, one was sitting on the couch, one was counting money, and the main guy was in the back room. Kenny immediately rushed to the back room to subdue the drug dealer, while Brother Mouzone and I watched the other two guys. There was a safe and a 30-30 Winchester rifle leaning right next to it. Kenny made the drug dealer open the safe, and we took a Winchester rifle and the contents out of the safe. Brother Mouzone and I gathered the money and drugs, and we exited the apartment. That day we hit the jackpot.

I had sold all of the guns I confiscated from the police officer's home except one, and I commenced to do robberies with a guy named Stanley who had just come home from prison. He lived with a woman named Marty, and although she was a beauty, she was just as thorough as any of the male hustlers I knew. Stanley and I did a lot of robberies, but one particular day he went to do a robbery without me, and he was caught. Marty and I continued to hang out together and we would visit Stanley at the Baltimore City jail. Stanley eventually was convicted and sentenced to 10 years imprisonment for the robbery.

Marty was also a drug user, so she and I started hustling together. She had a low-cut Afro, and once she put on a hat, she had the appearance of a dude. We robbed a corner store together and I was really impressed watching her. Marty

60

was twenty-seven years old, and I was almost seventeen. Then, there was honor among thieves, and I broke one of the cardinal rules, and that is never hookup with your buddy's woman, especially if he is in prison.

Marty and I started having sex and she exposed me to sexual acts that I have never experienced before. The intensity of having an orgasm with her vibrated through my entire body, and I became hooked.

We became a couple, and I eventually moved in with her. She had two boys, and I was three years older than her oldest son. She also had a brother living with her as well. He was a police officer with the Western police district who snorted heroin. On a couple occasions, he would take me out searching for women so I could snatch their pocketbooks while he waited for me in his car around the corner. I had just snatched a pocketbook and upon our return to the apartment, we noticed that the police were in the back of the apartment. Marty's brother went out to investigate. He showed them his badge and they immediately dispersed.

Once Marty and I became a couple, I was really astounded about how good she took care of me. Some of my older friends would make attempts to get with her, but she was loyal to me. They would even say to her that she was babysitting being with me. She would tell me every time someone would approach her, but I never confronted any of them. They started calling me a young gigolo.

CHAPTER TWELVE
Tragedy Strikes Again

One Saturday morning after leaving Marty's house, I went home to ask my mother for a couple of dollars. My sister Pat was doing her usual Saturday morning cleaning of the house, I don't really remember where the rest of my siblings were. Mr. George had become an alcoholic and was somewhere up the street drinking with his alcoholic friends. I was thinking that my mother was just relaxing in her room, so I knocked on her bedroom door and heard no reply. I continued to knock, it suddenly dawned on me that my mother never slept this late. I proceeded to enter her room, and she was lying in the bed and appeared to be sleeping. I shook her in an attempt to wake her up, but there was no response. My mind could not grasp the possibility of her being deceased. So, I continued to shake her, praying that she would wake up. A devastating feeling of deep distress came over me, and I yelled a loud piercing cry. My sister Pat rushed up the stairs to investigate. Once she realized what had occurred, she became hysterical. After she regained her faculties, she immediately turned her attention towards me, blaming me for all of the sleepless nights my mother spent worrying about me.

Donald Smith

My sister literally said that I was the cause of my mother's death, without actually saying those exact words. I started to internalize the words she had spoken coupled with the traumatic event. I actually began to blame myself for my mother's demise. If only I was the son, she could be proud of, instead, I was a sixteen-year-old drug addict who literally worried her to death.

My brother Larry was notified, and he was also devastated as he and I went to tell our brother Clarance. Clarance worked as a manager at a Giant Supermarket. As Larry and I drove to his place of employment, we discussed the unbelievable event that had occurred. I am sure that we both were in the first stages of grieving, which is denial. As we entered the store, we saw Clarance attending a customer. He was stunningly surprised to see us, but once he saw the expressions on our faces, he immediately knew something was wrong. We told him the tragic news; he wailed loudly in a moanfull cry as he went limp and fell heavily to the floor.

When my other brothers Marvin, Sylvester, and my sister Carolyn arrived, there were neighbors gathering in front of our home. A burst of anger emerged from within me, and I immediately when outside yelling in pain for everyone to disperse. Finally, Mr. George arrived, and he was intoxicated. I could smell the scent of alcohol as he spoke. Shortly after the coroner arrived to take our mother away, my siblings and I were utterly bewildered about what had occurred.

During my mother's funeral I was high off heroin because it suppressed my ability to feel the pain of losing her and the self-hatred I felt. My siblings, grandmother, aunt, and uncles were looking at me in disgust because of the lifestyle I chose to live. Or maybe I was just paranoid and up in my head about the shame I was feeling. Either way after the burial there was a repass and the atmosphere was a little uncomfortable because I would feel the awkwardness in my family and relatives when they interacted with me. Again, maybe it was my guilt that had me assuming that everyone was against me.

Somehow Child Protective Services became involved, and they had a discussion with my family about the possibility of placing me and my younger sister into foster care. My entire family said absolutely not, and my sister Pat took on the responsibility of becoming the guardian of me and my sister Carolyn. Pat was in her mid-to-early twenties when she took on this huge responsibility. At this time, I was living between Marty's house and my sister's. Pat became aware of my affiliation with Marty, and she was furious, especially about the substantial age differences. My drug use increased and my methods of obtaining drugs became more and more egregious. My capacity to care for others or to have sympathy had become numb.

I became diabolical in my efforts to obtain money to feed my drug habit, and my sister could no longer tolerate my behavior. Even though she never asked me to leave, I could see the sorrow and disappointment I caused her. So, I decided to leave because I no longer wanted to carry the burden of causing her frustration. I was always welcome to visit, and sometimes I would stay overnight.

My brothers Larry, Marvin, and Clarance had all moved out to their own places prior to me leaving. My brother Clarance was beginning to excel in his craft of selling large quantities of marijuana. Marvin had moved back to Castle Street with his children's mother Cynthia. Larry had met a woman named Deborah, and they decided to live together. Carolyn, Pat, and my nieces resided in the home.

CHAPTER THIRTEEN
Pennsylvania Avenue: A Whole New World

I was greatly astonished by how Marty was supportive of me through my ordeal with my family. I began to experience negative emotions like loneliness, isolation, abandonment, and rage that had profound effects on my behavior. My drug usage had increased exponentially, and my street behaviors would become outrageously dangerous. I literally didn't care about my life and no one else's.

Although I was seeing Marty, I was having a triangular affair with her, Jackie, and Yvonne. Jackie and Yvonne were wholesome women, and both of them had really supportive families. My children were very fortunate to have families who were responsible and participated in raising them. I was too irresponsible and caught up in the clenches of active drug addiction and street life. My addiction wouldn't allow me to do anything other than feed it seven days a week.

Yvonne had a job working at Stella Maris, it was a nursing home and hospice for well-to-do families. Like clockwork, I would meet her every payday, and she would give me money to purchase drugs. She never questioned me about my activities. Eventually, I stopped having sporadic visits with Marty and moved in with her permanently.

We would continue to hustle together, she swindled guys for money and drugs, and I continued to hustle in any way I could to obtain money. She was originally from West Baltimore and the areas surrounding Pennsylvania Avenue. Although I heard about the historic Pennsylvania Avenue, I didn't realize how it was known internationally for its entertainment clubs back in the 1940's, 50's, and 60's. There were the Royal Theatre, The Sphinx Club, The Redd Foxx Club, The Arch Social Club, and the Regent Theater. Entertainers like Billy Holiday, Nat King Cole, Louis Armstrong, Duke Ellington, Redd Foxx, Cab Calloway, Moms Mabley, and many more performed in the various clubs on Pennsylvania Avenue.

She knew hustlers, con artists, pimps, prostitutes, and guys who had the gift of gab who hung out on Pennsylvania Avenue. The first time she took me to Pennsylvania Avenue, I was mesmerized by what I saw. There was a full gamut of criminal activities going on right in broad daylight. People were shooting dice, drug dealers and pimps were immaculately dressed, wearing silk and wool pants, silk shirts, Homburg hats, and alligator shoes. There were guys playing three-card monte, drug addicts, prostitutes, and a lot more going on. Marty knew quite a few of them. Although I was perplexed about what I was seeing, I felt an attraction to that lifestyle.

Prior to coming to Pennsylvania Avenue, my entire world was the Wilson Park area, approximately a 10-block radius. I would occasionally go on missions outside of the area to obtain drugs or participate in a robbery. Marty had never revealed this side of herself to me until now, and I discovered that she herself had the gift of gab. She had introduced me to a brand-new lifestyle of crime that I hadn't been exposed to.

The attraction of Pennsylvania Avenue had inspired me to become more skillful in using underhanded tactics to feed mine and Marty's addiction. Marty and I became a dynamic dual of criminal activity, flim-flaming people. Because Marty knew a lot of hustlers and drug dealers on Pennsylvania Avenue, some of them would become our prey. They knew me as Marty's son, she would target hustlers who were at the top of their game, proposition them to come to her home for sex.

Prior to them coming to the house, Marty would notify me to let me know what time they would arrive. I would be in the house hiding and the guy wouldn't know I was there. After they had participated in their sexual activities, she would suggest that they enjoy a shower together. While they were showering, I would come out of my hiding place and thoroughly rummage through the drug dealer's pockets. I found a bundle of money with a rubber band wrapped around it. I would take only large bills like 100's, 50's, or 20's, and return to my hiding place.

The guy had so much money that he didn't have a clue that some was missing. Marty walked him to his car, and he casually drove away. This occurred numerous times with different guys, some of which would have bundles of heroin in the glove compartment of their cars and Marty knew it. I would take their car keys while they were in the shower, and I would search through the glove compartments and the trunks. I would take one bag out of each bundle, return the keys, and return to my hiding place. This activity went on for quite some time. We hit the jackpot several times without ever being caught.

We befriended an older gentleman from Pennsylvania Avenue known as Baltimore. I am sure that he got that name form being in Federal prison because in there, guys are from all over the United States and usually guys would be given the nickname of where you're from. Trust me, I know. Anyway, he was really inconspicuous in the way he did things and moved strategically through the streets; he avoided attention at all costs. He taught me the advantages of being semi-transparent and cautious while in dangerous drug areas and observing my environment at all times. He was a very charismatic person and inspired me to incorporate some of his savvy street ways. He must have been an old gangster in the past because drug dealers would sometimes give him heroin without him paying. When he would spend time with Marty, afterwards he would leave us enough drugs to last us for the rest of the day.

Before we devised a plan to swindle the guys, Marty's brother had moved out, and her children spent the summers with their aunt. I didn't give it a second thought about Marty being with those guys because my only objective was to feed my drug addiction by any means necessary.

We always found ways to get opioids, and Marty knew a friend who had lived in DC. He told us about a doctor in Washington DC named Dr. Moore, who ran a pill mill. He gave out methadone pills to treat drug addicts for a fee. We traveled to DC and arrived too early at Dr. Moore's clinic. It was 1971, and the movie Shaft had just come out. We had time to kill, so we went to a nearby movie theater and saw Shaft. When we returned to Dr. Moore's office, it was a line of addicts a block long. So, we got in line, and surprisingly it didn't take long to enter the clinic. It was a shabby looking office, and there was a man inside with a shotgun carefully watching everyone. When we entered a second room, there was another man collecting money and giving out numbers to be called. Approximately 20 minutes later, I was called to see Dr. Moore. He asked me why I was there, and I said because I have a long history of substance abuse and came to get some help with detoxing. He gave me a small medicine bottle filled with methadone pills, and I left his office. Marty and her friend went through the same procedure, and afterwords we headed back to Baltimore.

CHAPTER FOURTEEN
A tragic Event

O ne tragic morning, Marty's oldest son was sleeping in his bedroom. Marty went to wake him up so he could get prepared for school. Although he was breathing, he wouldn't wake up. Suddenly, Marty was inundated with fear as she rigorously shakes him. The ambulance came and they were unable to wake him as well and quickly rushed him to the hospital. He remained in a coma for a day or two. When he finally awakened, he was diagnosed with moderate retardation. The doctors explained that his brain didn't get sufficient amount of oxygen and caused brain damage. Marty asked the doctor about the cause of this tragedy, and he said the cause was unknown.

Marty's family assisted her with establishing services with the Kennedy Krieger Institute. They specialized in working with children and young adults with disabilities due to brain injuries, spinal cord, and musculoskeletal issues. Marty treated me like I was just a regular boyfriend, overlooking the obvious age differences between us. Her family appeared to have no issues with it because they knew that Marty was going to do what she wanted regardless of other people's opinion. They knew about Marty's lifestyle, and they only interacted with her in times of emergencies, but her oldest sister had always been supportive of her, especially her children. Throughout this ordeal, we managed to find ways and means to satisfy our drug addictions.

Marty and I continued on our journey doing whatever we could to satisfy our drug addiction. Although it seemed like we never had bad days, oh but we did. There were mornings when we woke up and our bodies were craving for drugs causing symptoms of aches and pains, tiredness, diarrhea, and thick mucus in the throat that causes a tickle in the back of the throat that you never can get rid of. I would always leave a little residue of heroin in the cooker (soda top) for just an occasion. We called it scraping the cooker. As soon as we were able to muster up enough energy, we would go out and hustle for enough money to soothe our cravings. As soon as the drugs would enter our veins, the symptoms of withdrawal would miraculously disappear.

We eventually moved to a newly built apartment complex called Sinclair Gates Apartment building on Bowley's Lane. I had no idea how Marty was able to obtain the apartment because neither one of us had a job. Marty was very instrumental in making things happen for us, and her phenomenal way of surviving in the drug game would sometimes astonish me. She always managed to make things happen for us. The surrounding neighborhoods were predominantly Caucasian and all I could see was opportunities to make money. I would stroll around the neighborhoods targeting women to snatch their pocketbooks.

Marty befriended a couple of ladies of the night who were just as savvy as she. Their names were Paula and Stephany who hustled in East Baltimore Street on the Block. The Block was actually two blocks of several strip clubs, sex shops, and other adult entertainment merchants. A lot of criminal activities occurred in the area, and ironically the Baltimore City Police Headquarters was literally located in the next block. The nightlife in Baltimore City was very surprising to me because I didn't realize how active people were throughout the night, and you could obtain any kind of drug of your choice even at two or three o'clock in the morning.

Money flowed into the block when Navy ships and longshoremen would dock at the Baltimore Harbor. Hustlers, strippers, drug dealers, and ladies of the night would capitalize on the abundance of opportunities to get money. Marty and I would go into our old bag of tricks of swindling Navy men and longshoremen out of their money. We knew that they were only docked in the harbor for only a week or two.

Out of the numerous times that we successfully executed our plan, there was one particular longshoreman who actually came back to our apartment to enquire about his missing money. We remained silent in the apartment while he angerly rang the doorbell and knocked on the door for approximately 30 minutes. He eventually left.

Marty would go out to do her thing and I would do mine. I always was good at burglarizing, and I was surveilling a bar around the corner from where we lived for months, and finally the opportunity came. It was approximately 3 o'clock in the morning when I made an entry through a small window that wasn't attached to an alarm. There were three cash registers, and they were filled with money. I gathered the money and made about three trips carrying bottles of liquor to the apartment. Marty and I were never drinkers, so we sold the liquor.

CHAPTER FIFTEEN
An Evening Excursion

I could always manage to gather together a stickup grew to hustle with, and two buddies of mine named Tyrone and Bo were always ready to rob an easy target. We had a third person, the getaway driver, when we saw a secluded pharmacy located beside a small acre of woods, it was the ideal target. There was a trail in the woods that lead straight to the other side of the next street over from the pharmacy.

Inside, there were two occupants when the three of us made our move. I pointed a sawed-off shotgun at the pharmacist and demanded that he open the safe. Nervously trembling in fear, he complied. We bolted through the wooded trail to our awaiting driver, who sped us away to the apartment.

We came away with a large sum of money that we divided among ourselves. One of my partners argued that we should have taken the drugs from the pharmacy as well. I explained that rummaging through medications would have cost us too much time, especially since we had no idea what we were even looking for.

About two weeks later, Tyrone and I decided to return to that same neighborhood to rob something—or somebody. It wasn't a good idea. This time, the neighborhood was on alert.

Donald Smith

Someone must have seen us and called the police, because when we spotted the flashing red, white, and blue lights, we ran. In the chaos, I hurled the sawed-off shotgun into the gutter as we tried to escape, but eventually, Tyrone and I were both caught. This time, the nature of the crime meant I was no longer considered a juvenile; according to Maryland law, juveniles who commit a felony can be tried as adults.

Once we arrived at the police station, Tyrone and I were placed in separate interrogation rooms. They grilled us about the pharmacy robbery — the pharmacist had reported that a sawed-off shotgun was used, and the police had recovered the weapon I'd tossed into the gutter.

I had plenty of experience with police tactics and the devious tricks they employed to force a confession. So, I kept silent, though I never knew what Tyrone was saying on his own. In the end, we were both charged with armed robbery and sent to Baltimore City Jail. The police claimed that the pharmacist had picked me out of a photo lineup.

At City Jail, I was assigned to the J section for juveniles. Yet, it was clear that there were adults in that section too, or at least men who looked like adults. It turned out to be the worst experience I've ever had — even though I knew a few people in that part of the facility. I was confined in an 8x10 steel cell fitted with steel bunk beds and a thin mattress. The toilet and sink were connected, so if you had to defecate, you were forced to do it in full view of your cellmate. The stench of someone else's filth was inescapable.

It was summertime, and the steel walls and bars absorbed the heat all day long. At night, I sweated profusely. It didn't help that I was enduring the worst drug withdrawal symptoms I'd ever experienced. By morning, my sheet and plastic-covered mattress were saturated with sweat. For nearly a week, I battled aches, pain, scorching and chilling bouts, and relentless diarrhea.

Most of my street smarts were useless when it came to navigating the unwritten rules of jail life. Still, my fierce hunger for survival kept me from becoming a victim of the madness that reigned there. I learned fast—or else I would have been swallowed up by the unwanted trouble that lurked around every corner.

I had been taught by Baltimore, from Pennsylvania Avenue onward, to be acutely aware of my surroundings, always sizing up who was neutral, who was weak, and who were the dominant troublemakers. In my cell block, there were two brothers; one was cool, while the other was pure trouble. I chose to remain neutral, never getting involved in the petty thefts of commissary or the predatory behavior toward the vulnerable. Some prison guards let certain inmates run amok in the cell block, while others were neither intimidated nor afraid. Those were likely the same guards who quietly brought drugs into the jail.

Being neutral meant minding your own business and sending a clear message to the fools: I would fight before anyone dared to disrespect me. On the inside, I was terrified, but I couldn't let my fear show.

One evening during dinner, as our cell block shuffled into the cafeteria to eat the so-called "slop" they served, I stood in the chow line and noticed two men staring at me. I met their gaze and immediately recognized them—they were the two men from the apartment that Kenny, Brother Mouzone, and I had robbed. They slowly approached and asked me about the incident, and of course, I told them they must have mistaken me for someone else. Later, I learned that they were in K section, the cell block right next to mine. Deep down, I knew it was only a matter of time before they confronted me. I could sense that they weren't buying my story.

During recreation in the courtyard, one of the men approached me, and I immediately saw that he had fashioned a makeshift knife. Before he could speak a word, I struck him. Of course, I ended up receiving a serious ass-whipping before the guards could break the scuffle. I don't know what happened to that knife, but I count myself lucky not to have been stabbed.

They took me to the prison infirmary, where a lieutenant questioned me. I was desperate not to be sent back to the J section cell block, so I told him that my life was in danger and that I couldn't return there. My body trembled with fear as I spoke. Keep in mind, I was only about sixteen and a half — looking much younger than my age. My terror was obvious, and the lieutenant appeared sympathetic enough to grant my request. I spent the next ten months in the M section of the jail, waiting for a court date.

I received occasional visits from my sister Pat, Yvonne, and, every now and then, Marty. I was glad that Pat and Marty never visited me at the same time; my sister detested Marty, and if they ever met, Pat would have probably attacked her. Pat blamed Marty for turning me out, but the truth was, I had chosen my own path.

Eventually, the visits from Marty dwindled until they stopped altogether. I wasn't upset — it was exactly what I expected. I had to be realistic about her struggle with drug addiction and understand that an addict's only focus is scoring drugs.

CHAPTER SIXTEEN
Hagerstown: An East Baltimore Reunion

O ne morning, my cell door opened, and the guard told me that I was headed to court. Even though I had been anticipating this day, I would've preferred to know a day or two in advance. I went to trial, received a five-year sentence, and was committed to the Maryland Department of Corrections. I was immediately taken to a monstrosity of a gray brick building called the Maryland State Penitentiary. The street side facing Eager Street was where the "committed" guys were processed and transported to their designated facilities to serve out their time, while on the opposite side and on the bottom row of cells were men serving 25-years-to-life sentences. I even saw a man named Mr. Hemphill from Wilson Park—he was there for killing his wife, serving a life sentence.

My cell door swung open as I headed to the chow hall for breakfast, and I heard someone calling my name. I thought, damn, I hope that isn't one of the folks I robbed in the past coming for revenge. To my surprise, it was Brother Mouzone wearing a Muslim kufi. He told me he was serving 25 years for armed robbery. After a brief conversation about how we both ended up behind bars, he tried to convert me to Islam while accompanying me to the chow hall. He had free passes to roam around the penitentiary doing his "Muslim stuff," and I attended a couple of religious services—mostly to get out of my cell.

During processing, I was designated for transportation to the Maryland Correctional Institution in Hagerstown. I felt a small sense of relief because I had heard so many horror stories about Jessup. Once I arrived at Hagerstown, it was late in the evening; I was processed and sent to unit 5. The cell wasn't as bad compared to City Jail or the Penitentiary, and I didn't have to share it with anyone. I had always been comfortable being by myself, ever since I was a child. Every night during lockdown, a speaker built into the cell wall played mystery stories. My vivid imagination found an escape in those tales, and every night, I would leave the confines of prison behind in my mind.

The next day, I was allowed out into the courtyard where most of the East Baltimore and Wilson Park criminals gathered. I saw Tyrone—the one I had done the pharmacy robbery with—James, who had given me my first shot of heroin, his brother Michael, Rodger (aka Hatchet), Black Timmy who sold drugs on Harford Road, a few guys I knew from Greenmount Avenue, Bo—also from the pharmacy robbery but there on another charge—his brother Billy, and others. In that moment, I felt right at home.

I was assigned to work in the cafeteria, handling kitchen duties, and I made juice for the entire facility at breakfast, lunch, and dinner. I saw everyone who came through the chow line, and I recognized most of them. The facility even had real silverware, and I managed to sneak a butter knife out of the kitchen. I sharpened it on the cement floor of my cell and hid it so that it wouldn't be found. I remained neutral while I was there, steering clear of unnecessary trouble.

There was a muscle-bound brother named Tyrone who constantly lifted weights and exercised. Also from East Baltimore and known to be a bully, he continuously harassed anyone he considered weak. One evening, coming from the chow hall, he decided to try me. He started an insignificant argument to disrespect me in front of other inmates. I kept my knife on me, ready for him if he ever got physical—although I hoped he wouldn't push it too far. With his shaved head and aggressive demeanor, I was prepared to jam my knife right into the top of his bald head if necessary. Both of us were very fortunate that day; had he reacted physically, I would have been charged with murder, and he might have ended up dead or paraplegic.

Years later, I saw Tyrone in East Baltimore, a shell of the man he once was. He was just leaving a methadone program and tried to hustle me for money. I told him how lucky he was that day in Hagerstown, and he just laughed it off. I handed him a couple of dollars and went on my way.

Every Saturday, the guards opened the entire unit so we could watch Soul Train. As soon as the doors opened, the guard would yell, "SOUL TRAIN time!" and everyone would race to the TV room to snag a front-row seat. We marveled at the beautiful dancers whose coordination and moves lit up the room as they strutted down the Soul Train line. The choreography was mesmerizing, and my favorite singing groups and solo artists—the Whispers, Luther Vandross, the Stylistics, Stephanie Mills, among others—filled the air with the popular songs of the 1970s.

Yvonne and my sister Pat would occasionally visit on weekends. I never got a visit from Marty, and Jackie would write often. Yvonne stood by me through every foolish situation I put myself in. In hindsight, I wasn't in love with Marty, but I definitely loved the way she cared for me and the things she did for me sexually. Hell, I was sixteen and didn't have a clue what love was anyway.

James and I joined the choir. I joined because I could sing and loved the sound of my own voice, while James couldn't carry a tune—he joined just to get out of his cell during choir practice and special chaplain events. One day, I was called to the chaplain's office, expecting choir business. Instead, the chaplain handed me the phone, and it was my sister Pat. She told me that our grandmother had passed. I pleaded to attend her funeral but was denied. At night, I'd reminisce about the good times with her as a child, the way she cared for me while my mother was in the hospital. She was a courageous woman, and I missed her dearly.

There was very little violence in the facility because Hagerstown had a gang of officers known as the "goon squad," and they didn't play. The entire staff of guards was Caucasian, except for one Black guy. Their reputation was well known among the inmates; the goon squad had a proven record of crushing any uprising or rebellious acts.

My stay wasn't as harsh as the months I had spent in City Jail during my five-year sentence. With cumulative good time added, I remained in Hagerstown for approximately two and a half years. I was then transferred to a lower-security facility, where I met one of the Veney brothers. Although he wasn't the actual shooter, he had been involved in the murder of a policeman back in the 1960s.

Eventually, I was sent to a halfway house on Greenmount Avenue and Eager Street. We occasionally got passes to step back into the community, and some of us even ended up at the free clinic messing around with some of the Latrobe project girls—I was one of them.

After about three or four months in the halfway house, I had a parole hearing and was granted parole under strict conditions: I had to report to a parole officer and submit regular urine specimens to ensure I wasn't using drugs. I thought that would be easy—I had been clean for years and was convinced I wouldn't go back to drugs. My parole officer even gave me an outdated Narcotics Anonymous schedule. Unbeknownst to me, every NA meeting I tried to attend was already closed. However, I did manage to pick up some literature about substance abuse and discovered that addiction is a chronic disease, much like diabetes or cancer.

Slowly, I began hanging around the same people and places, doing some of the things I used to do before my incarceration. I recalled Albert Einstein's definition of insanity—"doing the same thing over and over and expecting different results"—and thought that I could stick with old friends without falling back into drug activities. That hope was short-lived, and before I knew it, I was using drugs again. It's funny how, when you first come home from prison, everybody wants to hand you free drugs; but once you become addicted, you're left to fend for yourself, hustling for your next fix.

I was still on parole and required to submit urine tests. One particular day, during a visit with my parole officer, I knew my urine sample was dirty. So, I devised a plan to get some clean urine and perform a switcheroo—but it didn't work. The guy who monitored me noticed the container was cold when he picked it up. My parole officer could've sent me back to prison, but instead, he gave me another chance. In fact, my parole would soon be over, and I would once again be a free man.

CHAPTER SEVENTEEN
Mind Games

The disease concept of addiction had lodged itself in my mind as I battled conflicting thoughts. Part of me longed to stay clean, while another part was constantly drawn to drugs. Someone once told me that addiction is the only disease that talks back to you—he called it "disease thinking"—and that voice dominated my every thought. When I first came home from prison, everyone complimented me on how great I looked. I was clean, with a glowing aura about me, but before long, I let the darkness of active addiction seep into my soul. That inner glow dimmed, fading slowly until it vanished completely. I learned the hard way that hanging out with old friends will get you high before you can even convince them to get clean.

I moved back into my sister Pat's house, where Carolyn and my nieces also stayed. Pat soon tired of my drug-addicted behavior. Our days were filled with verbal confrontations, and eventually, I left—though she never really asked me to go. I didn't know where I would stay, but I was confident that my friends would let me crash at their places. I had no desire to search for Marty; I wasn't looking for her. Pat even let me come over just to shower and put on clean clothes.

In truth, I was homeless by my own choosing, drifting from one temporary refuge to the next. I even stayed with a guy I'd mentioned before—the one in the penitentiary for killing his wife—along with three or four of his children, who were also using drugs, and we'd occasionally hustle together. I also found shelter at Herbert's place, known as Fingers, though I never understood why folks called him that.

Soon enough, I was sleeping from pillar to post—wherever someone was willing to let me stay. At the same time, my brother Clearance was living in the St. George Apartments not far from Pat. He was housing our Uncle Paul, who was going through a major divorce. Out of options, I asked Clearance if I could stay at his apartment. He reluctantly agreed on one condition: I had to leave the apartment every morning when he and Uncle Paul left. He had every right not to trust me, and I accepted his terms.

When I arrived at his place, I discovered pounds of marijuana stashed around—it was nothing short of a stash house. As far back as I could remember, Clearance had always been hustling. Uncle Paul was there to keep an eye on things while Clearance conducted his business. I soon learned that Clearance was also selling hallucinogens—LSD, window pain, mescaline, and small pills called microdots. I steered clear of those psychedelic drugs because heroin was always my drug of choice.

Though I knew Clearance didn't fully trust me, I managed to convince him to let me sell marijuana for him. At first, things went great—I was selling and bringing him money. I spent every dollar I made on getting drugs, until my addiction worsened, and I became my own best customer, using his money to get high as well.

Through it all, Yvonne remained my steadfast support, regardless of my sleeping with other women or my criminal misdeeds. She cared for me without question, never prying into my business. Yvonne still worked at Stella Maris, and on December 28, 1976, she gave birth to my third child, Lakesha. I eventually convinced her that we should get a place together. I wasn't exactly working in a pie factory, but we moved anyway. Our son Kevin stayed with his grandmother, while Lakesha came with us.

My sister Pat later moved to Cherry Hill and convinced Yvonne and me to relocate there because the rent was affordable. We ended up on the same block as Pat, and I landed a job at a lumber company in Towson. An elderly couple next door fell in love with our daughter Lakesha; they took care of her so well that we never had to worry about a babysitter—she practically lived with them.

Even as I worked at the lumber company, my addict mind was always scanning for opportunities to feed my habit. I noticed one particular customer who made frequent trips to the lumberyard—he must have been a contractor given the volume of materials he purchased. Over days and weeks, I befriended him with casual talk until I felt comfortable enough to pitch him some deals on lumber prices. He took the bait, and for a month or two, I made a lot of money by selling him the most expensive materials for less.

Then, somehow, the administrators caught wind of my side hustle and set me up. Over the span of two days, a Caucasian man and two attractive Black women came through the lumberyard, placing orders while engaging me in friendly conversation. On the third day, the white man approached me with a couple of hundred-dollar bills, asking for lumber and other items. I took the bait, and about three hours later, I was called into an administrator's office. When I arrived, the same man was already there with an administrator smiling. The administrator requested to see the bills I'd received. As I handed them over, I noticed that the hundred-dollar bills were marked. I was caught red-handed and terminated immediately. Left with no choice, I fell back on my old criminal behaviors to support my drug habit and help Yvonne with our bills.

Pat had friends on the same block, and she introduced me to one of her girlfriend's husbands—John. The instant I met him, my internal addict sensor went off. It's amazing how one addict can recognize another; no matter where you are in Baltimore City—or anywhere in the world—you can tell when someone's in the same game, knowing where the best drugs are.

John's wife owned a car, and he would drive her to work, keeping the vehicle until she was picked up later. But it turned out that John was a notorious stickup guy, and he lived right across the street from me. One morning, after John had dropped his wife off, he came to visit. We talked about hustling, and out of nowhere, he pulled out two 9mm guns, handed one to me, and said, "Let's go." We spent the day riding around Baltimore City, scoping out businesses to rob. We hit three businesses that day and then immediately went off to buy drugs.

As we continued our robberies, John began taking increasingly reckless risks—risks I wasn't willing to follow. I had reluctantly agreed to help him rob a community agency. It was near closing time when we entered the front office wearing masks. There were about five people inside—four women and one man. We took all their possessions and made our escape. Later that day, while I was watching TV high on drugs, I caught a news report about the community agency robbery. I knew it was the place we had hit, but in my drugged state, I barely registered the report.

The following week, John wanted us to rob the rental office of the apartment complex where we lived. I was dumbfounded when I heard his suggestion—it was the beginning of the month when most residents paid their rent. John asked me one more time if I wanted to go along, and I said no. The next thing I knew, police sirens were wailing and helicopters were circling the neighborhood. John had robbed the rental office and gotten away. About a week later, someone identified him as the culprit; he went to court and received a 20-year sentence.

After about a year, the commute from Cherry Hill to Hunt Valley for work became too much for Yvonne, so her mother convinced her to move back home with Lakesha. I managed to secure a job as a groundskeeper—thanks to a friend of my sister's—at the apartment complex where we lived, and I rented out a room to help cover the bills. I continued using drugs, and miraculously, a dealer moved in right next door on the second floor. It didn't take long to connect with him; the quality of his product was top-notch. Eventually, I got fired from the groundskeeping job and went back to hustling—always searching for ways to make a dollar to feed my habit and pay the bills.

I later discovered that Yvonne's sister's boyfriend sold marijuana, so I convinced him to let me sell on his behalf. He would provide me with a couple of pounds on consignment, and I'd pay him after I made the sales. Hustling marijuana and managing my roommate's rent kept me in the apartment for about six months. During that time, I even started trading marijuana for heroin. One day, two hustling buddies came over to exchange some weed for drugs. After using the drugs, they drove me home. I was so high that I forgot I had left some marijuana in the car. Of course, I knew they were going to sell it. My marijuana connection was over, and I couldn't let that incident pass without taking action.

I knew where one of the two guys who had taken my marijuana lived. Two days later, I asked a female friend to drive me to his house—she had no idea what I was about to do. Once we arrived, I told her to park around the corner. I rang the doorbell, and the guy's sister answered. I asked for him, and after a moment, he appeared at the door. I plunged a butcher knife into his chest and ran to the parked car. I calmly got in, and the driver sped away. She never asked any questions about why she'd driven me there.

I later heard through the grapevine that the man I stabbed was taken to the hospital—and he survived.

CHAPTER EIGHTEEN
The Bank Withdrawal

It became too difficult for me to pay rent and support my drug addiction. Yvonne and I continued to see each other, and all the while I was trying to convince her that we should get another apartment together. Right before I was evicted, Yvonne, Lakesha, and I moved into an apartment on Midwood Avenue—right across from my old high school. Although Kevin would visit, he remained at his grandmother's house. I continued to hustle and occasionally contributed to paying the bills.

A friend of my brother Larry named Curtis approached me with the idea of robbing a bank. Now, I had never hustled with him before, but I rarely turn down an opportunity to make money. He told me he was going to get his mother's car and pick me up. I advised him to steal some license plates and swap them with his mother's plates. When he arrived, I assumed he had made the change. We targeted a bank in the county. Once we arrived, we didn't notice anyone outside the bank. We entered, and I immediately approached the teller, demanding large bills. She complied, but I noticed she had placed a dye pack in the bag. Curtis acted as if he were filling out a withdrawal slip, and when he saw that I had the money, we both raced for the door. I threw the dye pack to the ground, and it released a cloud of red smoke as Curtis and I jumped into the car. As we drove away, I noticed an elderly couple sitting on their front steps. I didn't give them much thought then, but later I learned they had written down our license plate numbers as we sped off.

Curtis never told me he hadn't changed the plates on his mother's car. As we casually drove away, county police were racing up the street while we cruised in the opposite direction. We arrived at my apartment and divided the money. That same day, I contacted a buddy named Duke, and we immediately caught the Greyhound bus to New York.

Duke had connections in New York, but outer towners had to be very cautious when traveling there—one could easily be robbed or come up missing. I hid the majority of the money at home; some of the bills bore red dye stains, and I used them to purchase our bus tickets and buy our drugs. We met up with a guy we both knew who had once lived in Baltimore. After picking up some heroin, we went to a shooting gallery—a dilapidated, abandoned building filled with at least 15 to 20 addicts. I was both bewildered and disgusted by what I saw. People were shooting heroin into open abscesses— into their necks, groins, even their penises. I managed to put on a façade and act as if this was normal, but inside I was astounded, struggling to keep from throwing up. We had to be super vigilant in the shooting gallery, because at any minute someone could try to rob you of your drugs. But once I managed to get the drugs in my system, all my inhibitions and doubts about the place disappeared. As always, the drugs took me outside of myself, offering a false sense of carriage and escape from reality. The next day, we returned to Baltimore. Rumors began circulating in the neighborhood that Curtis and I had robbed a bank. Aside from me, there was only one other person who knew this information—I never speak of my unlawful acts. Curtis ran his mouth before he headed to Denver, Colorado, where he stayed with relatives. The rumor eventually reached a guy known for robbing people. I knew of him, though I never really established a relationship.

One evening, while Yvonne and I were in the apartment, I heard someone knocking at the door. When I opened it, a masked man rushed in and placed a 9mm gun to my head, demanding money. I flat-out denied having any cash, so he locked Yvonne and me in the bathroom and began ransacking the apartment for valuables. Yvonne was terrified, and I did my best to assure her that it would be over soon. As she gradually calmed down, I focused on the masked gunman. Suddenly, it all clicked—I recognized him. It was Rod, a stickup guy I'd known.

After approximately fifteen minutes, I heard the apartment door slam. Although I knew him as a robber, his approach was amateurish. For one thing, you never leave your robbery victims locked away in a separate room, because you never know what they might do to botch the job. And secondly, you never leave the scene without getting exactly what you came for. I had plenty of experience with professional stickup men, and Rod was definitely an amateur. We cautiously emerged from the bathroom, and I noticed that some of my newly bought clothes and even my alligator shoes were missing. He hadn't found my hidden money stash, but he did take what I had in my pocket.

Even though I recognized the robber, I didn't know where he lived. After a bit of detective work, I found out that Rod lived on Old York Road, close to Willow Avenue. I asked around in the neighborhood, and everyone directed me straight to his house. I approached his home with a gun concealed at my waist and knocked on the door. A young lady answered, and when I asked for Rod, she told me he wasn't home. I searched for him for a couple of days, but he was nowhere to be found. I even contemplated throwing a Molotov cocktail through his window, but I couldn't risk hurting his family. Soon enough, word spread that I was searching for him, and I never saw him again after that robbery.

Approximately one month later, I befriended the neighbor who lived downstairs on the first floor. He told me his job was hiring and offered to arrange an interview with his manager. I did the interview—and to my surprise, I got the job, even though I was still using drugs. It was at an auto parts warehouse that distributed supplies all around Baltimore City and county. My neighbor was the delivery driver, and I filled orders for customer pickups and unloaded incoming trucks of auto parts. My criminal instincts kicked in as I watched the daily operations of the warehouse, and my conniving mind began to plot.

I slowly groomed my first-floor neighbor into joining me in a scheme to steal parts. When he loaded trucks for deliveries, I would slip 10 to 15 car starters onto the truck. During his routes, he would stop at the apartment and drop them off. I had a connection with a guy who owned an auto repair shop, and he would buy all the car starters we could gather.

Every so often, I'd hear rumors that the FBI was coming to Curtis's mother's house looking for him. I worked at the warehouse for about three months when one day the FBI came to my job and arrested me. Curtis's mother had convinced him to turn himself in, tired of the FBI constantly showing up at her home. He did so—and he also told the FBI that I had been with him during the bank robbery. At the preliminary hearing in Federal Court, I was surprised to see my supervisor from the auto warehouse speaking on my behalf. The judge released me under strict conditions: I had to go to work and come straight home. I was flabbergasted, but it happened.

Needless to say, my neighbor and I continued to steal auto parts. Approximately two weeks after returning home, the owner of the warehouse had an investigator follow my co-worker during his deliveries. We were caught and fired. I had violated my court conditions and was arrested once again.

CHAPTER NINETEEN
The Second Time Around

Once again, I ended up in Baltimore City jail. This time I was on a section strictly for Federal offenders. It wasn't long before I went to court. I was assigned a public defender who was really on his game. He visited me and disclosed all the evidence the government had against me. Including the fact that Curtis was willing to testify against me so he could receive leniency from the court. So, my attorney arranged for a plea deal of 8 years imprisonment. He explained that I should take the deal because with Curtis testifying against me during a trial, I could receive a lot more time. So, I took the deal.

The Federal system's waiting time to go to court was short, but getting to my final destination was hell. I was sentenced to spend my time in Morgantown West Virginia. It took approximately a month and a half to get there. Me and a bus load of other convicted felons were transported to a Federal facility in Newport Virginia and stayed there for two weeks. The next stop was Petersburg Virginia, and we stayed there for most of a month.

When I finally arrived in Morgantown, I quickly realized that it was a medium level security facility. There were no walls or barbed wired fences, just a lot of land and trees. Everything was immaculately clean, the lawns were nicely groomed, there were two tennis courts, a nice gymnasium, and the living quarters were nice as well. The place was populated with a lot of DC guys, and I eventually met one guy from Baltimore named Gary. By this time, I knew how to function in a prison environment, and I got along with everybody.

In the Federal prison system, there are different security levels of facilities. There are maximum, medium, and minimum levels. If someone was committed to a maximum facility, in accordance with their behavior while incarcerated, they could work their way to a minimum level. That is if they haven't been sentenced to life without the possibility of parole. I was really fortunate to have been sent to a medium level because most of the inmates were coming to the end of their 25-to-30-year sentence who worked their way to this level.

After about 30 days, I was assigned to work in the visiting room. My primary responsibility was to keep the visiting room clean. Most of the time I watched TV. I enrolled in school to study for my GED, and also took an architecture course because it was the closest thing to drawing. After I received my GED, I enrolled in college courses through the University of West Virginia, but people on the outside were protesting about how easy prisoners had it while incarcerated. So, a lot of programs geared to rehabilitating inmates were discontinued. Including the college program.

Eventually, Gary and I became good friends. I started hustling in the form of drawing portraits for inmates for profit. As time went on, Gary and I arranged for his girlfriend and Yvonne to come and visit us. Although Gary's girlfriend was attractive, I noticed that during our visits how fixated he was on Yvonne, but I shrugged it off as being nothing. Occasionally, Gary would have his girlfriend bring us marijuana, and sometimes heroin. I would hide the drugs in the visiting room, wait a couple of days, and retrieve the drugs during my working hours. Gary and I were really discreet about not telling anyone about having and using drugs. One evening, I was careless and was nodding in the TV room while under the influence of heroin. I noticed a fellow inmate who awakened me just before the officer came into the room. I quickly got myself together and went to my room.

Gary and I became really close, and we practically did everything together. It was rare to see one without the other. Gary was serving a lesser sentence then I, and after about a couple of years he was released. Although we vowed to keep in touch with each other, I didn't hear from him until years later.

For some reason the federal prison system administrators suddenly and unexpectedly transported me and several DC guys to another facility. It was approximately a bus full of us that were flown in handcuffs and shackled to a Federal Prison Camp in Pensacola Florida named Eglin Air Force Base. The prison camp was attached to the Eglin Air force base. It too was a minimum-security prison. The majority of the population were drug traffickers, white collar crime, corporate embezzlers, and racketeering. There were a lot of Hispanics there, and former Maryland governor Marvin Mandel who was convicted of fraud and racketeering was there as well. Me and the DC guys were definitely out of our comfort zone. But for a brief moment I thought that I could befriend one of the drug traffickers and gain a connection once I was released. But reality set in, and I realized that every time I tried to sell drugs, I became my best customer. It would be the equivalent of a monkey trying to sell bananas.

Like anywhere else, I made the best of my stay at Eglin. Approximately six months after I arrived, all of my DC buddies were being transferred to a coed federal prison in Lexington, Kentucky. Most of them were sentenced because of drug involvement, and it was stipulated by the courts that they receive drug treatment during incarceration. I was furiously angry because they were going to a coed prison without me. About 5 months later, I started writing to the court explaining that I had a long history of substance abuse, and there was no substance abuse programs in Eglin for me to attend. Three months after continuously writing to the courts, I was called to the administrative office and was told that I was being transferred to Lexington. Boy was happy.

A week later, I received a set of civilian clothes, a bus ticket, and about seventy-five dollars in cash for food, and I was driven to the bus station. I was amazed that they would let me travel alone—escaping never even crossed my mind.

It was a long grueling ride. There was a layover in Tennessee, and boy wasn't I happy. A guy approached me and asked did I wanted to buy some marijuana, and I said sure. I gave him 10 dollars and he handed me the bag. I went into the restroom to check it out, and the bag was filled with tree stems and dried grass. All I could do was laugh. Homeboy got me just like I got numerous people in the past. I just purchased some food and waited for the next bus to leave.

CHAPTER TWENTY
Prison Paradise

Even though I was given enough money to catch a cab, I intentionally arrived in Lexington, Kentucky completely broke. So, I called the prison to send someone to pick me up. Approximately 20 minutes later, a correctional officer arrived and transported me to the prison. It was a combination of a hospital and a prison. The hospital serviced inmates in the federal system who are experiencing serious medical complications. Once I was in population, the DC crew welcomed me.

There were inmates from all over the United States. This place was incredible for a prison, there was rolling skating once a week, basketball games between the University of Kentucky and the inmates, recreation rooms, a courtyard with tennis courses, and there were live entertainment events frequently. Of course, the women had separate housing units, but women and men participated in everything else together. You could also have 10 dollars in quarters. I would spend the next 5 years in prison heaven.

For some reason, I always seemed to attract older women. A savvy woman from Detroit named Sheila approached me one day, and we struck up a casual conversation. It was clear she was older and had seen tough times—she had been incarcerated for possessing a large quantity of cocaine. Her street dialect and mannerisms reminded me of Marty. Over the days that followed, we grew very close and spent nearly every day together, despite older men trying to intervene, much like what happened with Marty.

In the prison, inmates had designated secret spots—known as "jump off spots"—where couples could have sex. These locations changed frequently, and you could only manage a quickie there because getting caught meant being transferred to an all-male or all-female facility. Sheila and I visited these spots as often as we could, and the thrill of sneaking around and the rush of adrenaline from not getting caught made the experience just as exciting as the act itself. She was really skilled at giving oral sex—though, compared to Marty, she was a close second. I continued to hang out with Sheila until she was finally released.

Everyone in the prison worked during the day, and I was assigned to work on the paint crew. We had the liberty to go anywhere in the prison facility but had to be accompanied by the officer running the paint crew. A girl named Vickie was also on the crew, and she was gorgeous.

The majority of the women there were incarcerated because they became involved with men who were into the street life and drugs. Vickie was there serving time because she was involved with a well-known drug dealer in DC. I later learned that she had a boyfriend on campus who was also from DC, but that didn't stop me from pursuing her.

As time went on, Vickie and I became really close and eventually she broke up with her boyfriend. We remained casual because I was seeing a woman from North Carolina, and she was a ride-or-die chick. She literally did everything I would ask her to. She did my laundry, purchased things for me from the commissary, and we had sex every opportunity we could. She was a master at giving fellatio. I've heard about women for the South and how they catered to their men. But if you crossed them, there would be consequences.

One morning after we had sex, she had an appointment for a checkup in the hospital and the physician found my semen inside of her. They pressured her to reveal who she had sex with, but she wouldn't. She was transferred to an all women prison. This was the perfect opportunity for me to hook up with Vickie. She was a wholesome young lady, and she didn't have any street mannerisms at all. It was hard to imagine that she was involved with a drug dealer, but I learned that you can't judge a book by its cover.

I started getting familiar with a lot of people from all over the state, and I knew everybody who was into something illegal. The administration allowed anyone who had any kind of talent where provided opportunities for developing those skills. I had two talents, drawing and singing. A group of inmates would give talent shows and plays for the population. I would paint backdrops as part of the scenery for plays, and me and three other guys established a singing group.

In both situations, I was locked in the theater to do the backdrops, and the group was locked in the recreation room so we could rehearse. We became really good and had a great repertoire of songs, but just like on the street, I would always become sidetracked with drug activities and the drug lifestyle.

There was a Caucasian guy from Florida who was a major cocaine dealer. He was able to continuously smuggle quality cocaine into the prison. Once the DC boys knew about him having the drugs, they would intimidate him to give them cocaine, and he was really generous with it. Because I was accepted by the DC crew, they shared cocaine with me. I really didn't care too much for cocaine, but I took it anyway. The purity of the cocaine was strong, and you had to be careful about the amount you consumed. The only way we could use the cocaine was to snort it. I hated snorting, and one day while working in the hospital painting, I stumbled across some syringes. The entire time I was painting, my mind was fixated on how I was going to steal the syringes. Of course, I was able to get them. Stealing was my profession.

One crazy night in the unit, there was an officer on duty who would sleep all night until his shift was over. The DC crew was pressing the white guy for some cocaine because the more he gave, the more we wanted. On one particlular day he gave us an ounce of cocaine and things got really wild. I was the only one who had two sets of syringes, and the crew invited me to join them. Although cocaine wasn't my thing, I participated in using it. It was high quality cocaine, and as soon as the ounce was gone, the DC crew wanted more. I don't know how much cocaine this guy had, but it must have been a lot. It was about 5 to 10 of us running around like crazy trying to obtain more cocaine from the white guy. I gave up and returned to my room and tried to go to sleep but the cocaine had me wired-up. I stared at the ceiling all night.

The next day, rumors about what happened were spreading around the campus. Approximately a week later, the authorities did a shakedown and found one of my syringes strategically stashed away in my room. I wasn't charged with having it because I had two other roommates, and they couldn't establish who the syringe belonged to. Eventually, the white guy from Florida was caught smuggling cocaine and transferred to a maximum security prison.

Time went on and I became really complacent. Who could complain about doing time with women, having occasional sex, living my dream performing as a singer, and having all of my needs met. My only concern was getting caught having sex and being shipped out, but we were really savvy with establishing jump-off spots. Although I missed being home, it really wasn't on my mind a lot because this became my new home, and I was content.

Eventually, I was transferred to a work detail that everyone wanted—an assembly shop for US Air Force jet parts that paid a remarkable $1.50 a day, the highest rate on campus. My job was soldering, and as we worked, speakers in the ceiling played music. Some days were dedicated to R&B, while other days featured country music. I even started to enjoy some of the country tunes and found myself singing along as I soldered.

There was one personnel officer in charge of managing the shop and supervising our work. Occasionally someone would distract him while couples would sneak into the women's restroom to have sex real quickly. We were aware that the manager couldn't or wouldn't go into the female restroom. There was one girl who must have been a nymphomaniac. She had a huge sexual appetite, allowing several guys to have vaginal and oral sex with her. I didn't participate because I wasn't into having sex with a woman after another guy had ejaculated inside of her.

I played tennis and basketball, went roller skating, practiced singing, and continued to do shows with the singing group. All of a sudden, I got a word that a guy from Chicago was selling heroin. Just knowing there were drugs on the compound had changed me into a totally different person.

Donald Smith

We were allowed to have ten dollars in quarters, but people had much more the ten bucks and it was even paper money circulating. I had about thirty dollars in quarters, and my buddy from North Carolina also had money. He looked and sounded like a slow country guy, but he had the gift of gab. He could swindle people out of their possessions with ease. His slow and ignorant persona was used as a façade to bait you into his schemes.

We got two ten-dollar bags of brown heroin to see how good it was. I still had one syringe, and after I injected the dark brown heroin, an intense feeling of euphoria came over me. I hadn't had good heroin in years, and I immediately acquired an obsessive attachment to that feeling again. It was like I picked up exactly where I left off before I was incarcerated. Because I was renting out my syringe, I was able to get high practically every day.

My buddy from North Carolina also worked in the soldering shop, and we devised a brilliant scheme. We took a tube the same size and roundness of a roll of quarters, filled the tube with solder. Once the solder hardened, we put it in the quarter rapper and placed two quarters on each end to imitate the full role of quarters. We had four rolls, he took two, and I had two. That same day we went separately to purchase the heroin, and it worked like a charm.

Eventually, the heroin stopped coming in and I realized that I was experiencing withdrawal. It wasn't easy going through withdrawal and putting on a façade that everything was alright. While experiencing the thick mucus in my throat, diarrhea, and stomach cramps I still had to do my daily routine in front of prison authorities. After about a grueling week, I started to feel normal again.

CHAPTER TWENTY-ONE
Karma Makes a Visit

My stay in Lexington became routine, I continued to see Vickie and we took advantage of every opportunity to have sex. I became complacent and really comfortable being there. I was known by everyone, and I knew who was connected to any illicit activities on the campus. Vickie was eventually released, but we kept in contact throughout my stay. In her absence, I started seeing this very attractive blond hair blue eyed Caucasian woman who was a little on the crazy side, but she had a real talent for giving head. Actually, she was the second best I ever had to this day.

Some women would cut a hole in their jeans were their vagina was located. They called them jump-off pants. They would wear pants with no underwear so their partners could gain easy access upon entering them.

One evening my Caucasian friend and I was having sex in a dark corner of a building. We had a lookout to notify us if an officer should come our way. We were notified that an officer was headed our way, but the notification was a second too late. An officer had noticed us from a distance and yelled, "hey you two come here". Fortunately, it was dark and close to the time when the compound was closing, and everyone had to report to their assigned units.

The compound was crowded, I ran through the crowd into my unit, went to my room, changed clothes, and immediately went back outside. I was having a conversation with some friends when I noticed the officer walking right past us. I don't know what became of my Caucasian friend, but I did see her the next day and we laughed about our close encounter.

Yvonne and I were continuously in contact with each other. To my surprise, she arranged a trip to Lexington, Kentucky to visit me. Years later, I discovered that Yvonne had travelled to Lexington with my old friend Gary. They stayed in a hotel together. He stayed at that hotel while Yvonne was visiting me. No wonder I didn't hear from him after his release.

In hindsight, I too was disloyal to my friend Stanley when he went to prison, and I ended up with his woman Marty. I had broken the man code, which is, never mess with your friend's woman regardless of the circumstance. Karma is real, and you will definitely reap what you sow!

Every time I had a parole hearing, I was denied. The parole board rationale was that I got my break in court when I was sentenced to 8 years. In 1982, I was transferred to a half-way-house in Baltimore called The Volunteers of America. It was operated by federal authorities. I was there for approximately 30 days when I noticed a familiar face. It was Curtis, the guy I robbed the bank with, and who was going to testify against me. The next day, the authorities transferred him to an unknown location.

I was assigned a counselor who found me a job with a scaffolding company. They had contracts with the federal government. The capital building in Washington DC was under construction, and the scaffolding company was under contract to scaffold the buildings. Actually, I hated that job because I was terrified of heights, but it paid really good, and I wasn't willing to work beyond two stories of scaffolding.

I was still communicating with Vickie. On occasions, she would come and have lunch with me during my lunch breaks when I worked in DC. She seemed dedicated to our relationship, and she took advantage of the opportunity to see me.

My brother Marvin was a Baltimore City fireman, and he was stationed near the halfway house. To my surprise, I was called to the front desk and there stood Marvin. I was really glad to see him. I wasn't aware of him running drugs for my brother Clarence at that moment. I later discovered that he had a crew of guys selling drugs in East Baltimore. We had a casual conversation about different family members and how they were doing. He left without mentioning a word about his involvement with my other brother Clarence's drug operations, but I would soon find out through other family members.

It wasn't long before I was back using drugs, and I hooked up with a shady character name Butch. I met him when I was on a weekend home visit at my sister Pat house in West Baltimore on Hilton Street. Butch mother lived right down the street from my sister, and I ran into him one day buying drugs. We started using drugs together despite the fact that they were giving random urine test at the halfway house.

One day, Butch and I had passes to go out into the community. We went to a drug dealer that Butch suggested. I gave him my half of the money, and he purchased the drugs.

When we arrived at the halfway house, he refused to give me my half of the drugs. I kept telling him to give me my drugs, and he just ignored me. As he attempted to leave, I told him that he wasn't going anywhere until I got my drugs. He didn't think I was serious until I took out my knife and told him that both of us were going back to jail because he wasn't leaving the building until, I got my half of the drugs. He saw how serious I was and finally relinquished the drugs and left.

I was getting out of hand with using drugs, so I decided to get some methadone to ensure that I wouldn't go through withdrawals. Well, the same week I drunk the methadone, I was called to give a urine specimen. I was caught off guard, and I knew that the test results were going to come back positive. Approximately a week later, as I was preparing to leave the building, two US Marshals came to transport me back to Jail on M section.

It took approximately two weeks before I arrived back in federal prison in Lexington Kentucky. I was gone only six months and was back again. Strangely, I was satisfied with being back. I felt a sense of importance there because I knew everyone, and everyone respected me. I was living my childhood dream of singing in front of a large audience, was privy to any drugs that was able to come through the prison and having the opportunity to have sex while incarcerated was definitely a plus. I was in my element, again.

A well-known drug dealer from Philadelphia was recruiting guys to work for him once he was released. He was meticulous about who he asked, and he actually was interviewing people asking them if they were married, had children, or was a loner. If you were married or had children, you weren't a candidate. However, if you were a loner, he would be glad to consider you. I wasn't interested at all.

In April 1984, when Marvin Gay was killed by his father, mostly everyone was devastated that heard the news. That was the same year that I was granted parole and released. I resided with my sister Pat, my sister Carolyn, and my two nieces. I had a parole officer who was giving me random urine tests. He gave me a small paperback book to read, I don't recall the title, but it changed my perspective about how I was living. I made a vigorous and honest attempt to stay clean. My parole officer gave me a Narcotics Anonymous schedule to attend meetings, and I found a NA meeting at the old Firefighter's Union Hall on Central Avenue. I attended the meeting, but I felt out of place and uncomfortable. At the same time, old friends who were still caught up in their addictions were trying to hang out with me. I finally gave in and was off to the races once again.

In 1985, I was really entrenched in drug addiction. I had a visit with my parole officer, and I had a suspicion that I would have to give a urine specimen. I had obtained some clean urine and tried to pass it in the cup, and the guy who was monitoring me caught me trying to pour the clean urine into the cup. He acted like he didn't see anything, but I knew he had. On my next visit with my parole officer, he told me that my urinalysis test came back positive. I was given an ultimatum to return to prison or go into a 30-day treatment facility. Of course, I chose the treatment, I only had six months left until I completed my entire 8-year sentence day by day.

My parole officer arranged for me to be admitted to an inpatient treatment center called Changing Point. I had no intentions of being rehabilitated, it was just my best option opposed to going back to prison. The nursing staff and some counselors saw right through me, but I did like the therapy groups and individual sessions. It allowed me to see some things about myself that I was totally oblivious to. It became so insightful that I started reliving some of my childhood trauma. The feelings became too intense, so I elected to shut down, not knowing that I would have to revisit those horrifying memories in the future.

There were two guys I knew from East Baltimore named Johnny Lyles and Robert Earl; Johnny was my roommate. An older Caucasian woman who was also an inpatient, kept flirting with me. I just couldn't figure out why I always seem to attract older women, but I always took the bait. We had conversations about our lives, and eventually, she became overly interested in me. She started showing me pictures of her children and expressing feelings of wanting to have sex. I had to put the brakes on that chick, but before I did, I allowed her to perform fellatio on me. After that, I stopped entertaining her interest and put a stop to her pursuing me. It was like she was desperate for love.

During my entire stay, I simply went through the motions as far as treatment was concerned. I was more interested in completing parole than anything else.

After completing the treatment program, I returned to live at my sister's home. I heard through the grapevine, that Yvonne and her sister Earline were living together in East Baltimore. I called myself trying to surprise Yvonne by showing up unannounced. Boy did I get the shock of my life.

Earline answered the door, and she immediately yelled out, "Yvonne Donald is here". Yvonne was in the next room, and she was hesitant to show herself. So, I proceeded to go to her. She was pregnant and was carrying Gary's baby. She started shaking and stuttering as she tried to explain herself.

Although I was totally crushed, I told her an explanation wasn't necessary, and I left. I later found out that Gary had turned Yvonne onto using heroin. I continued to communicate with Yvonne because we had two children together.

Somehow, I miraculously made it through the last months I had left on my sentence, even though I was still using drugs. Through all the ups and downs, Vickie and I continued to communicate, and we started seeing each other regularly. I made a trip to DC to meet her son and family. She had a large family living in an urban section of DC. I was well received by her family. Vickie and I stayed the night at a hotel having sex and talking about old times in Lexington.

After my visit with Vickie, she started coming to Baltimore to see me on the weekends and would stay until the next day. Well, in the meantime, my sister Pat introduced me to her co-worker named Jackie. She was tall, slim, and an attractive brown skinned young lady. We started hanging out, and the first time we had sex, Vickie came unannounced to my sister's house. I don't know who let her in, but she came upstairs and saw Jackie and I lying in the bed together. She immediately turned around and left. That was the last time I saw or heard from her.

Jackie and I continued to see each other, and we finally became a couple. Although I was still using heroin, I tried not to break the law, but it was nearly impossible. I obtained a job threw Jackie's sister's boyfriend at the Baltimore Spice company. I was good at getting jobs, but I couldn't keep them to save my life.

I was assigned to the 3 to 11 shift, and I hated it. But Jackie and I had obtained an apartment in West Baltimore. My brother Larry and his girlfriend lived right behind us in the same apartment complex.

Donald Smith

I worked the 3 to 11 shift for a while and eventually I was transferred to day shift. All the while, I am still getting high. My mind was wired to seize any opportunity to make money to feed my desire for drugs. I worked formulating cure for meat, and it requires certain chemicals in the ingredients.

After every batch of our "cure," I had to take a small sample to the lab for analysis, ensuring the chemical mixture was correct. One day, as I entered the lab, I noticed several women's handbags on a lower shelf. My mind immediately began devising a plan to get the valuables hidden inside.

That same day, while I was taking my sample to the lab, I noticed that nearly everyone was out to lunch or caught up in a staff meeting. Seizing the opportunity, I quickly rifled through two of the handbags, grabbed the cash inside—nearly $200—and left the lab in a hurry. I didn't stop to think about the consequences; I just needed money for my addiction. It was like I was on autopilot, unable to resist the chance to obtain cash for drugs, even at the risk of getting caught.

At work, a loan shark would lend me money, but at 75 cents on the dollar. In other words, for every dollar he gave me, I had to repay him a dollar and seventy-five cents. Before long, I was deeply in debt, unable to borrow any more money until I paid him back—a debt I never cleared.

I can't remember how long I worked there, but as I sank deeper into my addiction, it became increasingly difficult to hold down the job. On a good day, I would manage to save some drugs for the next morning so I could get to work on time and perform my duties.

Yet, I couldn't sleep knowing drugs were waiting at home. It was as if my addiction had its own mind, commanding me to use them immediately. I obeyed without question—I couldn't have drugs around me unless every ounce was in my system.

I couldn't stop thinking about what was happening on the streets without me. The call of the streets, a world I'd known since childhood, grew stronger. Eventually, I gave in to temptation, started arriving late to work, and sometimes didn't come at all, until finally I was terminated.

Though I always managed to land a job, hustling was in my DNA. I was out of work for about a month, and during that time I went on a rampage. I reconnected with some old stickup buddies, and we got to work. One of them had been watching a drug dealer and discovered where he kept his stash. As soon as we arrived at the location, we were ready to pounce.

At the stash house, the buddy who had been surveilling the dealer knocked on the door while my other friend and I waited on the side. It was a textbook setup: someone looked through the peephole, recognized the visitor, and opened the door. We quickly overpowered the two men and the woman inside, gathered them into one room, and I kept watch while my buddies searched for drugs and money. It wasn't hard to find them—they were busy bagging drugs. While I was keeping an eye on the captives, I started flirting with the woman and making sexual gestures toward them. As we left the apartment, I even tapped one of them on the butt before we walked out. It was a successful hit—loads of drugs and cash in our haul.

CHAPTER TWENTY-TWO
Revengeful Sex

I continued to use and contribute anything I could to assist Jakie with the bills. One day while hanging out in East Baltimore. I decided to stop at a fast-food store to purchase something to eat. Lo and behold, there was the same woman in the apartment I robbed approximately two weeks ago.

When she saw me, her face had an expression of horror. After she realized that I wasn't there to rob the place, she settled down, and we started to have a casual conversation. We talked about how frightened she was when I robbed the apartment, and she asked me why did I touch her on her butt? I explained how I couldn't resist that gorgeous ass of hers. She smiled slightly as we continued to talk. She told me she was the manager of the place and lived in Lexington Terrace projects in West Baltimore. I became curious about how she managed to be at the apartment that particular evening, and she said she was there with her boyfriend. It appears that she was turned on by the intensity of the robbery experience and the attention I gave her during the robbery. When I left the store, I had obtained her contact information.

Donald Smith

At first, I thought that the number she gave me was bogus, but to my surprise when I called her, she answered. That day, we talked for a while and planned to hookup that following weekend. The weekend came and I purchased a room at the North Avenue Motel. Prior to checking in, I had used heroin, and it gave me the ability to sustain prolonged periods of sexual activity. We proceeded to have sex, and after about 20 minutes into it. As she was having an orgasm, she tearfully started saying "please don't leave me, I need you here with me".

I disregarded her statement because I too was about to have an orgasm. Afterwards, as we lay in the bed together, staring at the ceiling in silence. Suddenly I realized the statement she made during sex wasn't about me. She was heartbroken over a breakup with her boyfriend, and in the misted of having an orgasm, in her mind, I was him. It was possibly over the guy she was with at the apartment. I really wasn't interested in knowing the details of her situation, but she briefly touched on it, and afterwards we continued to have sex.

I wasn't concerned at all about her breakup, I love revengeful sex. Revengeful sex is when you casually meet a woman who man has cheated on her, or she experience an unexpected breakup, and they seek revenge by having sex with someone else. It is easy the spot those type of women by their conversations. They have ulterior motives, and that is to have revengeful sex with another guy. We met once more after our first sexual encounter and after that, I never saw her again.

There was a new hotel opening up on Baltimore Street named The Lord Baltimore Hotel. I attended the hiring seminar given by the hotel, and out of a lot of people who applied, I was one of them that was hired. At this stage in my life, I desperately wanted to get away from the streets and try to live a normal life. I wanted so desperately to stop using heroin, so I took my syringes and cooker and placed them in the trashcan outside of my townhouse. The very next day, I obtained some money, and I frantically ran outside to the trashcan, hoping to retrieve my drug paraphernalia. Miraculously, they were still there, and a sigh of relief came over me. I was really sincere about stopping, but I didn't have a clue as to how. The disease of addiction had a firm grip on my mind, body, and soul.

I started working at the Lord Baltimore Hotel in 1986, and the staff were mostly women. I was a houseman, and my duty was to bring all of the supplies the ladies needed to clean the hotel rooms, and vacuum the hallways of the hotel etc. At that time, I still had that magnetic pull of attracting older women. There was a housekeeper named Denise, and there was no doubt that she was smitten with me. I played the cat and mouse game with her, until we ended up going to her home to have sex. We even had sex in the hotel rooms where we worked. She was really good at hiding the fact that she was an alcoholic. As soon as I discovered she was an alcoholic, I left her alone immediately.

I hated being with women who were under the influence of any mind- or mood-altering substances. Besides Marty, all of the women I was in a serious relationship with were wholesome women and never used any unlawful substances.

I became a functional addict Everywhere I went, I would always search for opportunities to make money to purchase drugs. I had befriended a maintenance man working at the hotel named Jerome. I always had an inkling that he was a drug user, and one day he confirmed it when I noticed him under the influence.

There were at least a hundred rooms in the hotel, and every one of them had TVs in them. But you needed a special device to disconnect them from an attached cable, and the person that I knew had access to this device was Jerome.

I was talking with Jerome one day while we were having lunch in the cafeteria. I spoke with him about devising a plan to steal televisions from the hotel. He reluctantly declined, but I convinced him to sell me one of the devices that disconnect the cables from the televisions. He agreed, and he also gave me a master key to unlock the doors to all the hotel rooms. It took me approximately a couple of days before I could devise a plan to confiscate televisions. There was an abundance of overtime, and I would volunteer to work because most of the staff would be gone.

In the evenings, I would go to each floor to collect the trash in a large ben. I would put trash at the bottom of the ben, enter a room, disconnect the TV, put it in a large plastic bag, and place it on top of the trash, and put more trash over the TV. Flat screen TVs weren't out yet, these were those big bulky televisions.

The dumpster where I had to unload the trash were located in a small alley. I would place the TV into the dumpster and return to work. Once I got off, it would be dark and there was very little lighting in the alley. I would walk around the block to see if anyone from the hotel was outside. Once the coast was clear, I entered the dimly lit alley and retrieved the TV. I would catch the bus with this big TV in a plastic bag sitting on my lap. Thankfully, I had only one bus to catch. Of course, this routine occurred several times, and sometimes I was able to have someone with a car meet me after work to get the TVs. It is absolutely astonishing what you would do to feed your drug addiction.

One afternoon while I was working, I was called to the housekeeping manager's office. I was nervous as hell, and I just knew that I was going to be fired. Thinking that I was seen stealing TVs on a surveillance camera or something. To my surprise, I was asked to accept a supervisor's position, and I would be in charge of all the housemen. A huge sigh of relief came over me, and I accepted the position.

Now that I had some authority, the women started flirting with me more so than when I was just a houseman. Of course, I had to take advantage of the opportunities, I secretly had sex with some of them without the others knowing. Then, a young lady named Tonya was hired. She was a wholesome young lady, but a little naïve which worked to my advantage. She held the position as the housekeeping secretary, and for some odd reasons, I had an attraction for her. It was something about the persona of her personality that attracted me.

It didn't take very long before Tonya and I started seeing one another. Because I lived with Jackie, I would visit her at her home and in the community. She lived with her parents and a couple of her siblings. I met her parents, brother, and a couple of her sisters. Mothers always seem to have intuitions, and they intuitively know if someone has a shady character. Maybe I was tripping, but I felt suspicious vibes radiating from her mother every time I was in her presence. She had every right to be suspicious of me. I always had ulterior motives, and they were to satisfy my selfish needs, regardless of what they were and what I had to do to satisfy those needs.

I always visited Tonya late in the evenings, and we waited until everyone in the house was sleeping to have sex on the couch. I don't know for sure, but I believe Tonya was a virgin.

On December 21, 1987, Tonya gave birth to my fourth child, and she named him James. I had no choice but to tell Jackie that I got another woman pregnant, and she gave birth to my child. She was devastated. Jackie wanted to leave, but somehow, I managed to convince her to stay. I noticed that she started going out with her girlfriends more frequently, but I was always focused on satisfying my need to feed my drug addiction.

I believe that women are much savvier than men when it comes to having an affair. I knew from Jakie's increased activities that she had at least one affair, but I got too caught-up into my own self to give her the attention she really deserved.

I continued on my journey of addiction, I stole, swindled, and connived my way into a bag or pill of heroin. Although it was difficult to work while having a drug habit, I continued to work at the Lord Baltimore Hotel for approximately a year and a couple of months. The housekeeping manager, Ms. Weaver, became fond of me, and she liked my work ethics. When I had drugs in me, I could work non-stop.

Ms. Weaver was a stout Caucasian woman who didn't take any mess from anybody. I always had an inkling that at some point in her life, she was somehow associated with the street life. It was her demeanor and the way she managed people.

Ms. Weaver eventually left the Lord Baltimore Hotel, and she was hired to manage the housekeeping and the laundry departments at the Renaissance Hotel. Approximately one month later, Ms. Weaver asked me to come and work for her again. I immediately took her offer.

The hotel was huge and was at the end of its final construction. Again, I was the supervisor of the housemen, and as always, my radar was activated to penpoint any opportunity to make a buck. I was given a walkie-talkie because the hotel was so huge.

The Renaissance Hotel was so big, I could be gone for a couple of hours, and no one would even know. The first thing I had to do was to familiarize myself with the entire building. If anyone needed me, I could be reached by walkie-talkie. I found a door at the end of a hallway that led outside and there were no surveillance cameras. That became my exit point every time I stole something.

The chief of hotel security was a retired police officer, and I knew he was associated with his old police friends. He was privy of information stored in the police database management system. After about six months of working there, the chief of security called me to his office and accused me of stealing things that came up missing. I stole so much I didn't know if it was me or not who took the items he was talking about, but I'm sure it was me. I became beligerent when he started questioning me about my past. I instinctively knew that he had information pertaining to my criminal history. I knew about police tactics and how they would ask questions that they already know the answers to. I continued to deny stealing anything because he had no proof. From that point on, I was being watched by the entire security staff which was hindering my hustle. I knew that my criminal record was shared with Ms. Weaver, but it didn't deter her from our working relationship. That's when, I knew for sure Ms. Weaver had some affiliations with street guys like me or she continued to associate with them. Eventually, I was fired by upper management because that security chief was determined to get rid of me.

I was back on the streets, doing what I knew best. In East Baltimore, I ran into an old friend named Melvin. Melvin and I had hustled together back in the day—he was even one of the two guys who once took my marijuana when I left it in his car. Although we hadn't seen each other in years, it felt like no time had passed at all because we clicked immediately. He had a huge amount of cocaine and gave me a package to sell. I wasn't really into the cocaine myself; I sold it and used the profits to fund my heroin habit.

One day, I decided to sell cocaine in my old neighborhood, Wilson Park, thinking it would be just like back in the day. But to my surprise, things had completely changed—the area was slowly being taken over by ruthless young boys.

I hooked up with another old friend, Michael, not knowing he had become an avid coke head. We went to his house so I could let him try the cocaine, but he quickly started freaking out. He began pacing up and down the steps, took his shirt off, and ground his teeth in agitation. Although I was skeptical about having him help sell the cocaine, I waited until he calmed down, and then we set off to sell the package.

Less than an hour or two after we sold the cocaine, plainclothes police suddenly appeared. They jumped out of a car, and I started running, tossing the remaining cocaine without knowing where it landed. I managed to put some distance between us until, suddenly, I was tackled—like a Raven's linebacker taking down an opponent. I didn't know where this guy came from; as I was wrestled to the ground, several police officers rushed to help. One of them placed his knee on my neck, scraping my face against the asphalt. I had a sinking feeling I was set up. Could it have been Michael?

When I arrived at the police station, my face was badly scarred. I wasn't given any medical attention—instead, they put me in an interrogation room. That's when I learned they had found the cocaine I had tossed. One of the interrogators, who knew me from my younger days, walked in and said, "Long time no see, Duck." I looked at him in disgust. This wasn't my first rodeo; before they could ask any questions, I immediately requested an attorney. They then charged me with possession of cocaine with intent to distribute. Approximately three hours later, I was transported to Baltimore City Jail. Back in a hot cell and going through withdrawals again, I couldn't shake the old saying from my head: "If you do what you always did, you always get what you always got."

CHAPTER TWENTY-THREE
A Temporary Release

I was sent back to J Section, but this time things were different. I recognized a few guys from my time in Hagerstown, including my juvenile buddy Barnett from Boys Village. He appeared to be running things in that section. After about two weeks of detention, the guard opened my cell and told me I was being released on bail. I was confused about who could have possibly paid my bail. At first, I thought it might have been my brother Marvin, but my family always warned me that if I ended up in jail for anything other than defending myself, I would have to face the consequences. So, I wondered—could it have been Melvin, the guy I was selling cocaine for?

I still had some cocaine stashed in my house, and I repeatedly tried to contact Melvin, but he had vanished. Later, I went to City Jail to retrieve some personal items I'd left behind. When I explained my business there, they opened a secure door and locked me in a holding cell. I kept asking why they were locking me up, and the guard finally said I had been released by mistake. I was completely stunned.

Donald Smith

While I was being searched, I realized I had cocaine on me. My mind raced as I tried to figure out how to hide it without detection. I managed to palm the cocaine as I handed my pants over to an officer, and when he returned them, I casually slipped the stash into my pocket while he searched me.

I was sent back to J Section, and the next morning everyone was asking what had happened. I told them that the police had kicked in my door and arrested me because I was released by mistake—I was too embarrassed to tell them the real truth. Later, I confided in Barnett that I had some cocaine, and I asked if he had a syringe. He replied, "Come with me." We went to his cell, and we shot up all the cocaine together. I ended up staying awake all night, even though I didn't really like cocaine.

About a month later, I went to court and was sentenced to six months. I had already been locked up for a month and a half, so six months felt like a mere inconvenience. I was sent to City Jail and assigned to the Y Building—a stark contrast to the rest of the jail. The Y Building had air conditioning and was immaculately clean. It was like a dormitory for inmates with low sentences, and we were put to work doing maintenance around the jail. I ended up on the paint crew.

One day, while the paint crew was walking through the women's section of the jail, I heard a familiar voice calling, "Hey Duck, what's up?" It was my old friend Ann, from Milton Avenue. I always liked her style—she reminded me of Marty, a street-savvy dope fiend who was more thorough than most of the guys I knew. Ann and I had one sexual encounter back then, but we remained friends. I later met the McCullough sisters through my old friend Melvin. The McCullough family home was a popular hangout, and I also ended up seeing a woman named Valores, who lived next door to them. Although Valores wasn't a drug user, she was attracted to bad boys despite being a wholesome young lady. I lived in Cherryhill at the time, but I often spent nights at Valores' house. She stayed in touch even while I was serving time in Hagerstown.

Eventually, I was transferred to a halfway house on Egar Street, where I was on work release. There, I met a fellow inmate named Charles, known as China-man because his eyes were slanted like a Chinaman's and his constant smile made him memorable. China-man and I got a job at Rockland Industries on Edison Avenue and Federal Street, working as custodians in a huge factory that turned cotton into linen fabrics. Our supervisor, Baxter—who had one eye—kept a close watch on us. I never asked how he lost his right eye. After about three months, China-man and I were nearing the end of our sentences. The six weeks I spent in jail waiting for my trial were added to my six-month sentence, and after four and a half months, I was released.

By this point, I was growing tired of the drug and street lifestyle, but I wasn't ready to let it go. I picked up right where I left off before incarceration, using heroin and finding ways to get more. After China-man and I were released, we started hustling together. He had extraordinary auto-mechanical skills and could fix any car problem. Whenever he saw a car stranded on the side of the road, he would stop to help, and most of the time, he fixed it.

Our hustle was stealing catalytic converters. Together, we must have stolen at least 50 to 75 converters during our time hustling, and China-man had connections with mechanics who paid top dollar for them.

Slowly, I grew weary of living this lifestyle, so I reached out to my old boss, Ms. Weaver, to see if she had a position available. To my surprise, she had secured a manager's position at the Harbor Hotel and hired me once again as a supervisor in housekeeping. I wanted to break away from street hustling—I just didn't want to go back to jail. To help me along, I joined a methadone program while working at the hotel.

There was one employee at the hotel who kept harassing me. I tried my best not to retaliate, thinking he might believe I was intimidated by him. I even went to his supervisor about his behavior, but he continued. Finally, I had enough. One morning, still angry over an argument with Jackie the previous night, I ran into the guy who had been annoying me. He said something derogatory, and everything went blank. Before he knew what was happening, I punched him in the face and kept hitting him until staff pulled me off.

A meeting was held with Ms. Weaver, the employee's supervisor, and me. As I tried to explain what had happened, I felt my anger rising—so much so that you could hear it in my voice. Ms. Weaver tapped my leg to calm me down and intervened on my behalf. The supervisor admitted that I had previously reported the employee's behavior and had even discussed it with him.

My job was saved, and I continued to work there until Ms. Weaver decided to start her own cleaning service. I briefly worked for her in the new business, but I couldn't manage both jobs—mornings at the hotel and late evenings with her. It became especially difficult because I started shooting cocaine along with taking my methadone. It was ironic because I never liked cocaine, but mixing it with methadone became another addiction.

Eventually, I left the hotel and went back to drinking methadone and chasing cocaine, hustling by any means I could. I applied for a job at a fabulous nightclub called Port Discovery—I can't even recall its name. I was hired, and true to form, I stole anything that wasn't nailed down. My co-worker was an older gentleman named Leon, who was at least 70 years old and truly an old-school G from back in the day. His mannerisms clearly showed he had lived the street life, and I later discovered that he was an active drug addict. We used drugs together occasionally, though I was always afraid he'd overdose in my presence.

The club had three levels, each with at least two bars. I'd arrive early before the bars opened, then scour the area for any unattended liquor bottles. I'd grab a trash bin with a large plastic bag and fill it with as many bottles as I could find. Later, I'd take the bag out behind the building to a dimly lit alley, and often, I'd catch the bus at 1 a.m. with that huge bag of liquor and whiskey in tow.

The next morning, I'd walk to the methadone program for my daily dose. One day, as I approached, I noticed a guy making a delivery at a nearby corner store. Suddenly, another man appeared, held a gun to the delivery guy's head, and demanded money. I just kept walking, pretending not to see anything. I got my dose, went home, and sold the liquor and whiskey—it was easy money. This became my routine for about two months until the club eventually closed for good.

CHAPTER TWENTY-FOUR
Sick and Tired of Being Sick and Tired

I was always able to get a job, but I just couldn't keep one. I discovered that the Sheraton Hotel was hiring and applied for a supervisor's position in housekeeping—and I got the job. At that point in my life, I was growing tired of conniving, risking my freedom, and chasing a feeling that I never seemed to capture. I even switched methadone programs from West Baltimore to East Baltimore. Every day, I would walk from the Sheraton Hotel to the methadone program located right across from Baltimore City Jail.

A year after I was hired by the Sheraton, I found myself doing things that made me wonder why I hadn't been fired. I was having sex with nearly every woman working in housekeeping, and somehow none of them knew about the others. Sometimes, I even had sex in vacant hotel rooms with some of these women.

One particular morning, while I was delivering supplies to a young woman cleaning a room, I noticed a sad look on her face. Within minutes, she began to talk about breaking up with her boyfriend because he had cheated on her. As she spoke, I could sense that she was burning for revenge. I pushed her supply cart into the room and placed a "Do Not Disturb" sign on the door. After an intense sexual encounter, we returned to work as if nothing had happened, and we never spoke about the encounter again. The benefit of such revenge-driven sex was that there were no strings attached— just two consenting adults using intimacy to soothe their hurt and lash out at their pain.

Four years had passed since James was born, and in the early months of 1990, I impregnated Jackie with my fifth child, Janiqua Dominique Smith. During those four years, I grew sick and tired of being sick and tired—of chasing and using drugs. One day, out of the blue, I decided to go to the Sheraton's personnel office to talk about my drug problem. To my amazement, the HR lady was very empathetic toward me; she revealed that she was a recovering alcoholic with many years of clean time. She arranged for me to go to a 7-day detox facility.

It was February 27, 1990, when I entered the Church Hill Hospital treatment center. Kicking a heroin habit was one thing, but kicking a methadone addiction was another challenge entirely. I was given Clonidine to help with the withdrawals. I spent days spewing fluids and enduring devastating stomach cramps. People from Narcotics Anonymous came in and held meetings; this time, I sat in the front, fully focused. I heard someone say, "Remember your pain of withdrawal, and know that you don't ever have to feel that way again." That statement gave me the strength I needed to push through those seven days.

When I was released, I didn't want to leave the treatment center because, for the first time in my life, I felt safe from using drugs. The facilitators at NA encouraged us not to attend the Greenmount Avenue meetings, but that only piqued my curiosity. The very first NA meeting I attended after my release was held on Greenmount. I was terrified to walk up Greenmount Avenue to the recreation center where the meeting was held. I used drugs in that area and feared seeing someone I knew who might offer me drugs. I knew I was vulnerable, fresh out of treatment, so I took an alternate route: I walked up Barkley Avenue and down 23rd Street to get to the meeting.

I was shaking as I climbed the stairs into the meeting room. I was scared of the unknown, but I was even more terrified of going back to using heroin because I knew I wouldn't survive out there. The drug game had changed dramatically—young, ruthless people now ran it, with no qualms about killing anyone who got in their way. When buying drugs, you had to be silent and in perfect order. Plus, the so-called heroin wasn't pure at all; it was labeled an "unknown controlled dangerous substance," meaning it was only about 10% heroin mixed with 90% other chemicals.

Despite my fears, I needed confirmation that this NA thing would work. When I entered the room, I saw faces from my past—people I had shot heroin with, guys I had been in prison with, people I had robbed, even the guy I stabbed. Many of these individuals I had thought were either in jail or dead were there, clean, well-groomed, and clearly changing their lives. That was all the confirmation I needed. NA truly worked, because even those I considered much worse than me were now staying clean.

In NA, there were all kinds of misfits—murderers, prostitutes, rapists, drug dealers, child molesters, con artists—and somehow, I felt right at home among them. They helped each other stay clean, going to any lengths to make that happen. The misfits of society fit right in at NA. Their simple but clever slogans—"An addict alone is in bad company," "If you don't pick it up, it won't get in you," and "Keep it simple, stupid"—were instrumental in my sobriety.

Though I was uncomfortable with hugging other men, people in NA welcomed me with open arms. I once heard someone say, "He would steal your money and help you look for it"—that was who I was. After the literature was read, the facilitator asked if any newcomers wanted to introduce themselves. Nervously, I raised my hand and said, "My name is Donald, and I am an addict with 7 days clean." The room erupted in cheers, with everyone shouting, "Keep coming back! Keep coming back!" That moment lasted about a minute, and for the first time in 23 years, I felt the warmth and acceptance I had been desperately searching for.

After the meeting, I was introduced to several people with substantial clean time. I had managed to stop using drugs without being forced. One guy, DeLaneo, had been clean for five years, which blew my mind. These guys invited me to hang out with them—they took me to Lexington Market, paid for my food, exchanged phone numbers, and even drove me to the 5 o'clock meeting on Greenmount Avenue. I was skeptical at first, having been taught in prison that if someone freely gives you things, you might be getting groomed for something else. But I was fortunate enough to stay safe.

After the 5 o'clock meeting, three NA members—Thomas, Bubby, and James—took me to two more meetings. I would arrive home around 10 p.m., but every moment spent in those meetings was worth it. I instinctively knew that NA was where I belonged. As I continued on my recovery journey, I made some truly good friends who would go to any length to stay clean. I also discovered that some people in NA, though they were able to stay clean, continued to be tied to the drug lifestyle, selling drugs and doing things contrary to the NA program.

CHAPTER TWENTY-FIVE
A New Beginning

As I continued to absorb the life-changing concepts of the 12 Steps and 12 Traditions, I became overwhelmed by a flood of suppressed thoughts and feelings—emotions I had buried for over 23 years. Every horrible thing I had done resurfaced, filling me with deep remorse and shame. Some memories were so terrible that I can scarcely speak of them. I began to feel like that little boy again—the one who witnessed his mother being doused with hot lye, the one who found her lifeless body in her bed, and the one who once begged her for money to buy drugs. I even blamed myself for my mother's death, believing that her endless, sleepless nights worrying about me had contributed to her loss.

Those dark emotions had been numbed by drugs, but now I was dangerously close to using again. I was desperate for relief, and I realized it was impossible to face this pain alone. When I shared my feelings with the group, they suggested I find a seasoned Narcotics Anonymous member to guide me through the 12 Steps. At first, I was skeptical about opening up to a stranger, about sharing secrets I had sworn to take to my grave. But I knew I had to choose between seeking help or reverting to my old ways of self-medication.

I was terrified of falling back into that endless cycle of obsession and compulsion—to use drugs by any means necessary, even if it meant hurting others. A friend introduced me to a seasoned NA member named Harold. He was a businessman who always came to meetings in a suit and tie—a sharp contrast to his life as an executive at the Housing Authority in Baltimore City. Despite living in a luxurious condominium by the Harbor, when Harold stepped into an NA meeting, he was just another recovering addict, taking it one day at a time. I later learned that Harold was homosexual, but his sexual preference never mattered to me; I was hungry for the knowledge of this new way of living. He sponsored a few men, including one named Rob, who was at the Changing Point Treatment Center in 1985 when I was there. Harold was strictly focused on recovery and never once behaved inappropriately.

His first suggestion was to read the basic text of Narcotics Anonymous from front to back. I was astonished at how precisely the text described my life as an addict, as if the author had witnessed every detail of my active addiction. I came to understand that using drugs was merely a symptom of a much deeper problem—one I had long been unwilling or unable to address. I remembered that the first time I injected heroin, the relentless turmoil inside me vanished, and I spent 23 years chasing that fleeting euphoria, never quite recapturing that initial relief.

I kept Harold as my sponsor until I outgrew the guidance he could provide. At that point, I reached out to a man named Artie—someone who lived, breathed, and embodied the 12 Steps. I asked him to be my sponsor, and he accepted. There were regular 12 Steps and 12 Traditions meetings adjacent to the main NA meeting at Greenmount, and Artie encouraged me to attend them to fully understand their purpose. With his immense knowledge, Artie took me on a deep, often frightening journey within myself that was ultimately both challenging and gratifying.

Eventually, I reached my fourth and fifth Steps. I was terrified of conducting a fearless moral inventory because it meant confronting the demons of my past—revisiting my entire life and sharing it with someone else. I feared judgment and looked down upon for exposing my truth, yet I kept hearing NA slogans like, "Your darkest secrets will set you free." The thought of returning to drug use was far more terrifying than facing my demons and sharing my story.

When I began writing my fourth Step, the pages overflowed with accounts of deceit, betrayal, and the many hurts and unsavory behaviors associated with my addiction. Yet, within that darkness, I also discovered hidden strengths— my creativity, reliability, hard work, and resilience. I realized that my lifestyle, my habits, my actions, my thought patterns, and my old friends were standing in the way of change. I had grown up in an environment where showing weakness was not an option. I had used my childhood trauma—my hurt, anger, and bitterness—as a kind of armor. In that state, I didn't feel weak; I felt powerful and strong. Acting on my negative emotions allowed me to hide my vulnerabilities, so I could hurt others without feeling a thing. I became a living testament to the saying, "Hurt people hurt people."

While writing, I discovered that everyone living that same lifestyle was driven by trauma, pain, and bitterness. The most dangerous person is often the most damaged, and I have met many dangerous individuals—people who would kill if you crossed them.

When I felt bitter and angry, I didn't consider that I was deeply wounded—physically, mentally, and spiritually. I maintained a façade because, in my world, showing weakness could get you killed. That disguise kept me safe, and I was terrified to let go of those negative emotions, for fear that I would become completely vulnerable.

The law of attraction is truly miraculous. I learned that, besides the father wound in my soul, I also carried a deep mother wound. My mother cared for me in ways that made me feel special, even when I behaved horribly. Losing her at sixteen left an intense longing for her motherly love and attention—a void that drove much of my behavior. I began to understand the human psyche, and how we constantly yearn to fill a specific need. The law of attraction doesn't care whether those needs are negative or positive; it makes sure our desires manifest. I grew skeptical about coincidences and came to believe that everything has a cause and effect. There is a common thread within us that attracts our specific needs, whether those needs stem from childhood trauma or other life situations. That emptiness in our souls subconsciously influences our behavior throughout our lives.

I now realize why I attracted older women when I was younger. It wasn't because I was some great, charismatic young man; it was an invisible force that drew us together for a common reason. They fulfilled my need for motherly affection, and I, in turn, met their unconscious need to be nurturing. Every encounter—whether with an older or younger woman—shared a common thread: both were trying to soothe a deep-seated need and feel validated.

My trauma took me on an unimaginable journey of substance abuse, criminal activities, incarcerations, destroying lives, and near-death experiences—all in a desperate search for a solution to heal my inner pain. It is frightening to look inward without an objective and strategic plan for healing. Confronting my inner demons through the 12 Steps has given me the courage to face my fears and view my trauma from a perspective of change.

The fourth Step was brilliantly designed for people like me—committed to change, yet aware that without this work, one would undoubtedly relapse. Doing a fearless moral inventory didn't erase the pain; it simply put things into perspective and helped me clearly identify the root causes and effects of my trauma. I began to understand that my past trauma directly influenced my present behaviors.

After completing my fourth Step, I was flooded with regret, remorse, hostility, and all the emotions I had suppressed for years. I felt like I was losing my mind, having never confronted those feelings without being under the influence. I felt vulnerable, but I knew that to survive without drugs, I had to share my experiences with my sponsor. That's when I moved on to the fifth Step.

I needed guidance, yet I was terrified of being judged for the terrible things I had done. When my sponsor and I sat down, I poured out secrets I had sworn to keep buried forever. As I spoke, the heavy burden of shame, guilt, hurt, and remorse began to lift, like a deflating balloon. My sponsor listened silently, his face unreadable. When I finished, he immediately took my written words, placed them in a metal container, and burned them. The ashes that floated into the air symbolized the release of my pain. Then he began sharing his own story—his experiences, strengths, and hopes—and explained how he had managed to heal some of his own deep wounds. He emphasized that this was just the beginning of a lifelong journey—a continuous cycle of falling down and getting back up, determined to maintain total abstinence from drugs and alcohol. We ended our session as we had begun, with a prayer. In that moment, I realized I had a huge responsibility: to nurture and heal the wounded little boy inside me.

CHAPTER TWENTY-SIX
Self-Discoveries

I was relieved when my session with my sponsor finally ended, and I felt a little lighter after releasing much of the emotional baggage I'd carried for over 23 years. I say "much" because a deep self-centeredness still lay at the heart of my disease—a trait Narcotics Anonymous taught me was a constant battle. In psychological terms, my self-centeredness is egocentrism, meaning I was always focused on satisfying my own needs. Hidden within that self-absorption was the vulnerable little boy who had witnessed his mother being doused with hot lye, the boy who found her lifeless body in her bed, and the boy who blamed himself for her death because she had spent many sleepless nights worrying about me.

For years, I suppressed those feelings with drugs, until I came dangerously close to using again. I was desperate for relief and realized I couldn't face that inner pain alone. When I expressed my feelings to my group, someone suggested I get an experienced NA member to guide me through the 12 Steps. At first, I was skeptical about sitting down with a stranger and sharing secrets I'd sworn to keep buried. Yet, I knew I had a choice: either face my feelings or revert to my old ways of self-medication.

I was terrified of returning to that endless cycle of obsession and the compulsion to use drugs—no matter the cost. A friend introduced me to Harold, a seasoned NA member who came to meetings in suits and ties. Harold was an executive at the Housing Authority in Baltimore City, living in a luxurious condominium by the Harbor, but when he entered an NA meeting, he was just another recovering addict, taking it one day at a time. I later learned Harold was homosexual, but that never mattered; I was hungry for any guidance on this new way of living. He sponsored a few men, including one named Rob, who was at the Changing Point Treatment Center in 1985 when I was there. Harold was completely focused on recovery and never once acted inappropriately toward any of us.

His first suggestion was simple: read the basic text of Narcotics Anonymous from cover to cover. I was amazed at how precisely it described my life as an addict—as if the author had observed every detail of my active addiction. I learned that drug use was only a symptom of a much deeper problem I had been unwilling or unable to confront. I remembered the first time I injected heroin—the relentless turmoil inside me vanished, and I spent 23 years chasing that fleeting euphoria, never quite recapturing that initial relief.

I kept Harold as my sponsor until his guidance could no longer help me grow further. By that time, I knew who truly embodied the 12 Steps, so I reached out to a man named Artie. He lived, breathed, and even slept the 12 Steps of NA. I asked him to be my sponsor, and he accepted. Artie advised me to attend the 12 Steps and 12 Traditions meetings held near the main NA meeting at Greenmount, so I could fully understand their purpose. With his immense knowledge,

Artie led me on a deep, sometimes frightening journey within myself—one that was ultimately both challenging and gratifying.

Eventually, I reached my fourth and fifth Steps. I was terrified of performing a fearless moral inventory because it meant facing the demons of my past—revisiting my entire life and sharing it with another person. I feared judgment and humiliation, but I kept hearing NA slogans like "Your darkest secrets will set you free." The thought of returning to drug use was more frightening than facing my past demons and sharing my story.

As I began writing my fourth Step, the pages overflowed with deceit, betrayal, and unsavory behaviors tied to my addiction. Yet within those painful details, I also discovered strengths—creativity, reliability, a strong work ethic, and resilience. I realized that my lifestyle, my habits, my thought patterns, and my old friends were all barriers to change. I had grown up in an environment where showing weakness was not an option. I had used my childhood trauma—my hurt, anger, and bitterness—as armor, which made me feel powerful, even though it allowed me to hurt others without feeling a thing. I became a living testament to the saying, "Hurt people hurt people."

While writing, I discovered that everyone who lived that same lifestyle was driven by trauma, hurt, bitterness, and pain. The most dangerous person is often the most damaged, and I have met many dangerous people—people who would kill if provoked.

When I felt bitter and angry, I didn't consider that I was deeply wounded physically, mentally, and spiritually. I maintained a façade because, in my world, showing weakness could get you killed. That disguise kept me safe, and I was terrified to let go of those negative emotions for fear of becoming completely vulnerable.

I also learned about the law of attraction—that in addition to carrying a father wound in my soul, I had a deep mother wound as well. My mother cared for me in ways that made me feel special, even when I behaved terribly. Losing her at sixteen left an intense longing for her motherly love and attention, a void that drove much of my behavior. I came to understand that the human psyche constantly strives to fill its emptiness, whether that need is positive or negative. The law of attraction doesn't care about the nature of your needs—it ensures that your desires manifest. I grew skeptical of coincidences and began to believe that everything has a cause and effect. There is a common thread within us that attracts our specific needs, whether those needs stem from childhood trauma or other life experiences, and that emptiness subconsciously influences our behavior throughout our lives.

I now understand why I attracted older women when I was younger. It wasn't because I was some great, charismatic young man—it was an invisible force drawing us together for a common reason. They fulfilled my need for motherly affection, and I, in turn, met their unconscious need to nurture. Every encounter, whether with an older or younger woman, shared one common thread: both parties were trying to soothe a deep-seated need and feel validated.

My trauma took me on an unimaginable journey of substance abuse, criminal activity, incarcerations, destroyed lives, and near-death experiences—all in a desperate search for a way to heal my inner pain. Confronting my inner demons through the 12 Steps has given me the courage to face my fears and view my trauma as a catalyst for change.

The fourth Step was brilliantly designed for people like me—committed to change, yet aware that without this work, relapse was inevitable. Completing a fearless moral inventory didn't erase my pain; it simply put things into perspective and helped me identify the root causes and effects of my trauma. I began to understand that my past directly influenced my present behavior.

After finishing my fourth Step, I was overwhelmed by regret, remorse, hostility, and all the emotions I had suppressed for years. I felt like I was losing my mind, having never confronted these feelings without the influence of drugs. I felt vulnerable, but I knew that to survive without drugs, I had to share my experiences with my sponsor—that's when I moved on to the fifth Step.

I needed guidance, but I was also terrified of being judged for all the terrible things I'd done. When my sponsor and I sat down, I poured out secrets I had sworn to keep buried. As I spoke, the heavy burden of shame, guilt, hurt, and remorse began to lift, like a deflating balloon. My sponsor listened silently, without judgment. When I finished, he took my written words, placed them in a metal container, and burned them. The ashes that drifted into the air symbolized the release of my pain. Then, he shared his own story—his experiences, strengths, and hopes—and explained how he had managed to heal some of his own deep wounds. He emphasized that this was only the beginning of a lifelong journey—a continuous cycle of falling down and getting back up, determined to maintain total abstinence from drugs and alcohol. We ended that session as we had begun, with a prayer. In that moment, I realized I had a huge responsibility: to nurture and heal the wounded little boy inside of me.

CHAPTER TWENTY-SEVEN
A Celebration of Life

All week long, I heard about a Narcotics Anonymous convention in Philadelphia and grew curious about attending my first NA convention, but I had no means of getting there. I was told to chase my recovery like I chased drugs, so I did. On the morning of the convention, I attended the 12 o'clock meeting at Greenmount Avenue. Confident that I would somehow make it to Philadelphia, I even carried a small travel bag with me. I questioned everyone I met about the convention, asking if they were going. Miraculously, a fellow member and his wife were planning to drive to the convention, and they needed a few extra people to share the expenses for travel and lodging. A couple of other members and I rode with them. I immediately let them know that I was completely flat broke, but as a newcomer, I didn't need any money—everything was covered by them. I relished the way NA members made me feel important and welcomed.

We arrived at the convention just in time to hear the opening speaker. The event was held in an enormous ballroom filled with thousands of recovering addicts from all over the country, and it was standing room only. I was mesmerized, overcome with overwhelming gratitude. Emotions surged through me—tears of joy streamed down my face, and I felt both jubilant and embarrassed. I had been taught that grown men don't cry, so I tried to hide my tears, but a couple of strangers noticed and immediately enveloped me in hugs, assuring me that it was okay to cry. I have never felt so welcomed and supported in my entire life, and to this day, the memory brings tears to my eyes.

After that euphoric experience, we encountered difficulties finding a room since all were booked. Fortunately, we reached out to some Baltimore members who had rooms available, and we were accommodated. About eight of us ended up sleeping in one room. I slept on the floor, close behind a woman I knew. Suddenly, I felt aroused by the gentle contact of her soft skin. I had a throbbing erection and made a sexual advance from behind. She wasn't aggressive; instead, she turned around and politely explained that while she was flattered, this wasn't the type of party we were there for. We were there to celebrate sobriety, and she helped me put things in perspective. We both turned away from each other and went to sleep.

The next morning at breakfast, I wasn't charged for anything. They even covered my registration, a comedy show, and a ticket to the dance. My prison mentality kicked in, and I became suspicious of their generosity. What could they possibly want from me when I had nothing to give? I shared my feelings with an experienced member, and he explained that all they wanted in return was for me to pass that generosity on to another newcomer whenever I could. He said, "We keep what we have by giving it away." I was a bit confused—how can you give something away and still keep it? Another phrase, "You have to surrender to win," also puzzled me.

Later, I came to understand these paradoxical phrases. In my journey to maintain sobriety, it became imperative to help others stay clean. One addict helping another is the fundamental principle of recovery. I learned that newcomers are the most important, as their struggles mirror my own. Recognizing these shared struggles keeps me vigilant; there is no recovery without sharing experiences, strengths, and hopes with another suffering addict.

After breakfast, we attended meetings throughout the day—there were numerous topic meetings, even marathon sessions lasting 24 hours during the convention. In every meeting I attended, the speakers seemed to speak directly to me. Although they lived in entirely different states, I felt as though they were talking about my own experiences. Confused, I turned to an experienced NA member for clarification. He explained that every recovering addict is connected through our shared experiences. When you hear people speak and feel as though they're talking specifically to you, it's because they are. Our shared struggles bind us together and enable our recovery. We depend on one another because our lives are at stake. One recovering addict knows what we have been through, and by sharing his or her experiences, strengths, and hopes, the therapeutic value of mutual support becomes clear. As the literature says, "As long as the ties that bond us together are stronger than those that will tear us apart, all will be well." I was blown away by his explanation—it made everything less confusing and clearly comprehensible. I realized how blessed I was to be there.

The next day, we attended a huge speaker's banquet. Everyone was elegantly dressed and greeted with hugs as they entered the grand room. I wore jeans, an NA T-shirt, and tennis shoes, yet at the ballroom entrance, I was embraced as if I were wearing an evening tuxedo.

After the speaker finished, people were recognized for their clean time—a celebration of the struggles we endured to achieve sobriety. It was like a countdown from 40 years clean to just one day. When your clean time was announced, you would stand up and be celebrated for every year, month, week, day, or even minute of sobriety.

At one point, the speaker asked, "Is there anyone with one day clean?" A number of newcomers stood up, and thousands of recovering addicts erupted in cheers. The sound shook the enormous ballroom as the newcomers were lifted onto the shoulders of other addicts and carried around, with chants of "Keep coming back, keep coming back" ringing out for at least 15 minutes. Tears flowed freely as we celebrated our hard-won battles against a mind-altering chemical that once destroyed our lives.

That jubilant experience filled me with gratitude for every time I had risked my life—being shot at, injecting drugs, engaging in unprotected sex without thinking about diseases like AIDS. It was all about self-gratification, taking what I wanted, when I wanted it.

This convention was a mind-blowing experience. It connected me to the true nature of my disease and taught me how to maintain my sobriety through the support of fellow recovering addicts. Once I returned to Baltimore, my buddy and I began spreading the message of recovery in jails and other institutions. This work continued for a couple of years until I became distracted from my primary purpose of reaching out to suffering addicts. Because of my addictive personality, I sometimes become addicted in other areas of my life, causing as much chaos as drugs once did.

CHAPTER TWENTY-EIGHT
My First Anniversary

Shortly after moving from West Baltimore to the East side, I celebrated my first year clean without a drink or a drug on February 27, 1991. Jackie, my sister Pat, and my daughter Janiqua, who wasn't even a month old, attended my anniversary. I spoke about my entire 23 years of addiction, and some of the horrible things I did. My sister and Jackie were listening and for a moment I regretted disclosing things that I thought would cause them to judge me, but it was imperative that I shared my experiences, strengths, and hopes. I was experiencing a high that drugs could never give me.

Afterwards, my friends and I went to O'Dell's Nightclub, and we had a ball. I soon discovered in NA when you're riding on cloud 9, and feeling enthusiastic about being clean, that is the most critical time of your recovery to remain vigilant. I became lackadaisical about working on myself because I thought that I had arrived. Gradually, I became complacent. Habits and behaviors of the past were slowly emerging without me even noticing it. I found myself in Lexington Market searching for women who were careless with their pocketbooks so I could steal their money. I started being

Donald Smith

unfaithful in my relationship as I was in the past and justified my behaviors by telling myself at least I am not using drugs. Yeah, I was clean, and I was living dirty.

I was taught that the disease of addiction is cunning, baffling, and insidious, and is the only disease known to man that speaks to you. It has you justifying the most outrageous nonsense in order to justify your behavior. But when you're full of yourself, the things you were once vigilant about tend to escape from your mind like Houdini. Self-gratifying pleasures with women took over me and my drug of choice walked through the doors of Narcotic Anonymous. She had a tall slender body, a nose ring, and spoke with a distinctive New York accent. I was mesmerized by her mere presence, and her beauty compelled me to introduce myself.

By this time, I had impregnated Jackie, and she was carrying my sixth child named D'Aris, and at the same time, I had fallen deeply in love with my drug of choice, my NA girl. She was a highly sexual woman and knew how to perform in ways that I haven't experienced since my old days with Marty. Even though she performed the same sexual acts I had experienced with other women, her sexual talents were more amazing. Was I in love with her or was I in love with the way she made me feel? I'm sure it was the latter, because I had no idea how to love at that point.

She had two boys and was residing with her aunt and uncle. I had decided to leave Jackie because I convinced myself that I was in love with another woman. I secretly obtained an apartment and moved out while Jackie was at work. To this day I still regret the way I left her. She was pregnant, working, maintaining the household, and providing for my daughter. She was an amazing woman. My guilt wouldn't allow me to see her, or my children struggle, so I made sure that they didn't go without anything they needed. She is a good and decent woman who didn't deserve to be treated that way, but all I was thinking about was me and my selfish needs.

At this point, I had gotten all of the flirtatious behaviors with other women out of my system. I was back on track with my recovery. My NA girl and her two children eventually moved in with me, and I quickly realized things are very different when you're living together. Slowly but surely her unresolved issues began to emerge.

I have heard several women's stories in NA, and I personally think most of the women lived horrific lives before and during their addictions. A lot of male and female children had to contend with being sexually molested by adults, and in some situations the maltreaters were family members and care providers. Traumatized children grow up to be traumatized adults, launching us into a never-ending cycle of searching for relief from our inner turmoil. Drugs had become a band-aid to numb our tormented souls that unresolved trauma had unleased within us.

During the progression of active addiction, prostitution becomes a reliable means of obtaining money for drugs. Men and women subject themselves to the most dangerous situations just for a moment of relief from their inner pain. Some of the most self-degrading sexual acts are performed by women and they are more likely than men to become victims of abuse and even death.

My NA girl wasn't exempt. She lived that lifestyle of prostitution and enticed men for monetary gain. It is impossible to live the lifestyles we live and not be affected socially, physically, emotionally, mentally, and spiritually. In recovery, it is crucial that those five dimensions be addressed because if you don't change, the same person will definitely use drugs again.

Once we stop working on ourselves, those feelings of self-degradation, low self-esteem, and negative self-regard start to surface. A rude awakening must occur to snap you back into reality. This is exactly what happened to me concerning my NA girl. I recognized her behavioral shifts because I experienced what noncompliance can lead to in recovery.

Opportunities to enhance my life were overlooked because I was comfortable with being average. Well, I wasn't settling for average anymore, I was working to become a better person to myself and others. I was doing things in this relationship that I had never done before like being monogamous.

I provided a stable living environment for my NA girl and her two children for three consecutive years. I worked as a Psychiatric Rehabilitation Counselor and worked the morning shift. She worked the 3 to 11 shift as a certified nursing assistant. I would cook dinner, clean, wash clothes, and make sure her children were safe. Once she arrived home, there was a hot meal waiting for her. Living in this way was something she had never experienced, and it was definitely out of her comfort zone. That uncomfortable feeling can cause irritational behaviors that will lead you right back to your comfort zone of settling for less.

She started zooming in on negative issues in our relationship without finding ways to resolve them as a couple. Regardless of all the right things I was doing as her partner, nothing was good enough. I remember one evening she was preparing to go out. She explained that she was going out with a friend she met in the NA fellowship, but I noticed that she was wearing brand new underwear and matching bra. She was being very meticulous about how she was looking. I concluded that she was going out to see another man, and my heart sank. I never confronted her with my thoughts, but later it was revealed that my suspicions where right.

Eventually my NA girl decided to move out into her own apartment, and I was completely devastated. I put my whole self into this woman and her children. Remember the verse in Marvin Gay's song Distant Lover when he said, "when you left you took all of me with you"? That is actually how I felt, empty. Never in my life had I experienced the gut-wrenching pain of someone leaving me. It was this excruciating pain piercing through the center of my chest, and I couldn't shake it. At night, I was curled up into a fetal position trying to rock with the pain in hopes that it would go away. I had unsuccessfully used self-soothing methods trying to regulate my raw emotions. Using was never an option, but homicide was.

CHAPTER TWENTY-NINE
Divine Intervention

I continued to maintain contact with her and went to visit her at her new apartment one night. She said I could visit but I planned to show up unannounced. My feelings were still raw, and my mind was repetitively thinking that she had male company. I grabbed a butcher knife and proceeded to walk towards her apartment. The entire time I was walking, my mind was in a fog. Although I knew where I was going, I don't remember seeing traffic or pedestrians. It was like I was in a trance and external stimuli just wasn't computing.

I concealed the butcher knife as I knocked on her apartment door. The moment she opened the door; I invited myself in searching for the presence of another man. Astonishingly, no one was there except her. Once again, a higher power was working in my life protecting me from myself. Chris Rock once did a joke about O J Simpson saying, "I don't condone people killing their ex-wives and boyfriends, but I understand." Those were my sentiments as well.

For days I was in a perpetual state of confusion and could not see the end of the tunnel. I only knew how to solve my inner pain by finding outside solutions, but I desperately knew that using drugs wasn't the answer.

Donald Smith

The intensity of the turmoil inside of me was truly unbearable, so I did what I always done my entire life, and that was to search for outside solutions for my inner turmoil. I thought by keeping her in my life in some way would help to soothe my abandonment pain. So, I proceeded to manipulate my way back into her life by trying to foster a friendship.

She allowed me to visit her and that some point, we even had sex a couple of times. All the while, my insecurities started to influence my thoughts and inundating my mind with the belief that she was seeing another man. I knew that she kept a diary of her daily activities, and she would keep it hidden within her apartment.

My primary mission was to obtain her diary to either confirm my suspicion that she was seeing someone or not. I managed to obtain her apartment keys and made copies to keep for myself. One day while she was working, I entered her apartment to search for her diary. After looking under her mattresses, I found it. I started to read its contents, and my worst fear had come to fruition.

She worked 3 to 11 shifts, and each night before coming home, she would stop at the house where the guy she was seeing lived. Suddenly I heard someone at the front door, it was her son coming into the apartment. I quickly placed the diary back under the mattress and headed towards the bathroom. Once he entered the apartment, I came out of the bathroom as if I had just finished using it. Of course, her son told her what happened. We saw each other a couple of times after that incident, and we slowly drifted apart. I was still seeking solutions outside of myself to alleviate my inner pain, so I sought religion.

Fragmented Memories of a Man Child

I was raised to believe in Christianity and the belief in worshiping God. A Narcotic Anonymous friend of mine was an avid church goer. He suggested that I accompany him to church services with him on Sundays. Although I wasn't into religion, I was searching for anything that could help relieve my pain.

I attended church for a while, and I even had a church home. But I couldn't shake that feeling of not fitting in. I felt like the people weren't authentic in the way that they interacted with me. It was like they were playing a role to see who could be the most religious.

I was reluctant to share my story of drugs and prison life because people in the congregation frowned upon that lifestyle. They were very judgmental even though most of them had an unscrupulous past themselves But what really turned me away from religion, is the action of the pastor. His mannerism and swag reminded me of a street hustler. He was married and proudly spoke about his first lady of the church on Sunday mornings. All the while, he was being savvy with the women of his congregation and was eventually caught sleeping with several of them. There were too many distractions, and I couldn't focus on my primary purpose, which was healing my pain. So, I returned to my place of refuge, Narcotics Anonymous.

I began to hear NA slogans repeatedly in my head like, "If you don't pick it up, it won't get in you," and especially "If your ass falls off, pick it up, bring it to a meeting, and we'll help you put it back on." So, I started taking my ass to meetings and sharing my feelings until I was able to muster enough energy to intensely evaluate my past actions. It was puzzling to me how something or someone outside of me could affect me to the point where I wanted to take a life.

I came to realize that my reactions had nothing to do with anything or anyone other than me. I have no control over someone's decision to leave me, but what I can control is how I react to it. After another serious and honest inventory of my past relationships, I discovered that I unconsciously placed my X-NA girl in the same category as my mother and my absent father, which I had never done before with anyone else.

I previously stated that I never experienced that gut wrenching pain inside of my chest, well in retrospect, I was wrong. That little sixteen-year-old who discovered his mother was deceased and who had a lingering desire to have his father in his life felt undesiring, left behind, insecure, and discarded. So, I had to do the math. Undesiring + left behind + insecurity + discarded = feelings of abandonment. My reactions of wanting to kill wasn't about anything happening outside of me, it was the inner pain and feelings of being abandon once again.

My ex-NA girl married another NA member who treated her in a way that was familiar to her. He continuously abused her mentally, physically, and sexually. Her inner trauma wouldn't allow her to accept a man who treated her with love and affection. Those two feelings were foreign to her, and she saught a relationship with features of a man she was familiar with. At one point she filed for a divorce, and it was granted. Approximately, one or two months later, she remarried the same guy. The definition of insanity is, "doing the same things and expecting different results". The abuse picked up right where it left off, but again she divorced him.

Years had passed and one day I ran into my ex-NA girl. When she saw me, she immediately started explaining how she never cheated on me, and how she wasn't ready to have a man like me. I understood perfectly what transpired between us and why. It was the universe revealing to us our self-destructive behaviors caused by our inner trauma that needed to be addressed.

It was foolish of me to think that my NA girl could reciprocate the love, loyalty, or the enthusiasm I gave to her and her two boys. Asking her for those things in return was beyond her capacity to give. How could she give me what she was unable to give herself? Realizing this fact helped me with my healing process.

CHAPTER THIRTY
Power of Examples

I never wanted to be in a position where my unresolved issues would drive me to kill someone. I turned to the Serenity Prayer, trying to embrace acceptance as a path to serenity. Yet, I had a tendency to try to control people and situations to satisfy my own selfish needs—even though my efforts were often futile. I invested great energy into changing my reality, but coming to the realization that I was truly powerless over people, places, and things was a long and arduous process.

For years, I manipulated my surroundings as a way of protecting my inner child. The simplicity of the Serenity Prayer always eluded my complicated mind. They say that Narcotics Anonymous is a simple program for complicated people. My inability to distinguish what I could change from what I couldn't only made my life more difficult. Instead of accepting reality as it was, I tried to bend situations to fit my own worldview. Now, I understand what the Serenity Prayer was trying to teach me: that accepting people, places, and things—and having the courage to change what I can—brings true tranquility. For me, that remains a lifelong practice.

I eventually realized I could no longer search for solutions outside myself to heal my troubled soul. Healing from my breakup was monumental, but each day, the pain in my wounded soul began to subside. I knew it was inevitable that I would see my ex-NA girl at meetings, and her mere presence would usually trigger overwhelming emotions. Finally, one day I saw her and felt nothing.

I worked hard to establish a conscious connection with a higher power, praying for the strength to transform my current occupational status. I was still working as a Housemen Supervisor at the Sheraton Hotel, but I wanted more. I knew that the only way to elevate myself was through education, and I had many examples in NA that showed me the way.

There was a former well-known drug dealer named Michael, now in recovery, who had been robbed by one of my stickup buddies during our days of active addiction. Michael resisted, and his right arm was completely blown off by a sawed-off shotgun. Yet, he showed an extraordinary example of forgiveness when, on his anniversary, he reached out to the very man responsible for his injury. Michael eventually became an adjunct professor at Baltimore City Community College and a passionate advocate for education. Another example was a female recovering addict named Veronica, who was so far gone during her active addiction that she talked to lampposts. In recovery, she earned three degrees. These two individuals profoundly influenced me. Although both are now deceased, they carried the message of recovery with them to their graves—and beyond.

I earned my GED while in Federal prison and then enrolled at BCCC. The NA slogan "you got to give it away to keep it" became ingrained in me, so I chose addiction counseling as my major. Getting through the required prerequisites was a struggle; I hadn't been in school for years, and algebra was completely foreign to me—I even had to take that course twice before I passed. Even on this righteous path, I battled constant temptations and struggled to resist my sexual desires.

I worked in the mornings and attended college in the evenings. In class, I noticed a woman who kept eyeing me. One evening after class, I introduced myself. She came off as warm and friendly, and we began talking frequently. Eventually, I started giving her rides home after class, dropping her off just around the corner from her house. Although she was married with two children, she appeared deeply unhappy. I was curious about her sadness but never directly asked about her marriage.

When she felt comfortable enough to open up, the floodgates opened. She spoke nonstop about her situation. Her husband worked for the FBI, but he wouldn't discuss his job specifics. She explained that while he was an excellent provider, he was also a womanizer and extremely critical of her. Suddenly, I had an epiphany: she was searching for relief from the anguish inflicted by her husband, and I was willing to accommodate that need.

One particular evening after class, she began exhibiting playful sexual behaviors toward me, and I could literally feel the intensity of her desire. Seizing the moment, I noticed an empty classroom nearby and immediately took her hand, leading her into the unlocked room.

The mix of excitement and the risk of getting caught only heightened the intensity. We passionately kissed until she abruptly stopped, crouched down, unfastened my pants, and enthusiastically began performing oral sex on me. The raw, unbridled pleasure she displayed was unlike anything I had ever experienced—it was as if she was releasing years of unmet desires from her unhappy marriage, and it left me craving more. Her unleashed sexual frustration was so exhilarating and fulfilling that future encounters became inevitable. Our sexual escapades continued every evening in my car until she eventually felt comfortable enough to visit me at my apartment.

After a couple of semesters, our classes diverged, and I began seeing another woman who lived not far from college. Occasionally, the married woman and I still had sexual encounters. I fell back into a pattern of having multiple sexual partners, as I had in the past. This is an example of how addiction can manifest in other areas of life—sex became a way to escape myself. It diverted me from my primary goal of inner growth, providing an artificial sense of accomplishment. Narcotics Anonymous literature warns, "One is too many, and a thousand is not enough." I found myself caught in that vicious cycle of addiction once again, this time without drugs.

CHAPTER: THIRTY-ONE
Establishing A Career

I changed careers and began working for an agency called the National Center on Institutions and Alternatives (NCIA). The co-founder was a recovering addict and former drug dealer—a devout Muslim who was highly educated and exceptionally business savvy. Besides Mr. Randy, he was the second Black man I had ever seen in a leadership role. His intelligence and distinctive articulation during agency meetings were impressive, and he quickly became one of my NA heroes. In him, I saw a symbol of my aspirations to become better educated.

At that time, the government had started de-institutionalizing all mental health facilities in Maryland, releasing men and women diagnosed with chronic mental illnesses into community psychiatric rehabilitation and residential programs. With government grants available for startup programs, NCIA was established. The entire agency was staffed by recovering addicts, and I seized the opportunity to join. I worked on the grounds of The Rosewood Center in Owings Mills, Maryland. Each of the three houses on the campus housed three residents, many of whom had dangerous pasts. One of my clients had killed a woman during an attempted rape, and I had to accompany him on weekly doctor visits to receive injections to curb his sexual urges. Another client, during a psychotic episode, had killed a man with a hammer. Even though both were heavily medicated, the staff had to remain vigilant at all times.

I grew to love working with this population and later changed my major to social work when I transferred to Coppin State University. My college years at Coppin were the best of my life, thanks to their superb social work program.

After working for NCIA for about three years, I secured a job at a Residential Mental Health and Psychiatric Rehabilitation Program called New Ventures. I was taking public transportation because my car had completely died. One morning, I noticed a familiar face from NA. When we started talking, I discovered she was raised in the Wilson Park area and knew my brother Larry. Although I was still seeing a married woman at the time, my new associate and I soon began a sexual relationship as well.

One night, during a phone conversation, our discussion shifted to her sexual preferences. She admitted that she loved having sex with both men and women, and immediately the wheels in my head started spinning. I asked if she had any experience with threesomes, and before long, I proposed a three-way conversation over the phone with her and my married friend. Eager to please, she agreed. During that conversation, she managed to convince the married woman to participate in a threesome, so I scheduled a meeting at my apartment. I hadn't expected the married woman to join, but I guessed she was exploring her newfound sexual freedom. When the three of us met, I sensed some initial apprehension in the married woman's demeanor, but my new friend helped her relax, and we indulged in a night of passionate, uninhibited pleasure.

After engaging in sexual activities with both women, I became preoccupied with watching them enjoy each other. I even captured moments of their intimacy on camera. Later, the married woman confided that she found it difficult to see me with another woman. I was confused, but I gave her words no further thought.

Over time, I became deeply intrigued by the complexities of my new friend's personality. Eventually, I let my guard down and allowed her into my heart, and once again, I found myself in a serious relationship with another NA member. Yet, my pattern of multiple relationships persisted. Soon, I became entangled with a woman whose unresolved trauma led her to seek solace through familiar, unhealthy behaviors. Despite the glaring warning signs, I walked down the aisle and said "I do." I even ignored the initial minister during premarital counseling who refused to marry us because he knew we weren't ready. Ultimately, we arranged for Father Sam—a Catholic minister in NA—to marry us, a testament to my persistence in getting what I wanted.

I gave her all of me in hopes that she would reciprocate, but three years into the marriage, we found ourselves on the couch discussing ways to end it. She revealed secrets that devastated me—she had been sleeping with other men, sometimes complete strangers, throughout our marriage. We agreed to file for divorce, but we remained friends.

Before our separation, I was selling clothes and traveling to New York's garment district at least twice a month to purchase clothing and women's handbags. I was doing well financially enough to buy another house with the intention of starting an assisted living home for mentally ill adults. Instead, I packed my belongings and moved into a house on Harford Road, leaving everything to her. We continue to be friends to this day.

Donald Smith

During her prostitution days, she gravitated toward Caucasian customers because they treated her kindly, while her Black customers were often abusive and dominating. When she remarried, she married a "Wigga"—a Caucasian who emulated Black culture—who was also a member of NA. He was a womanizer, and his family wasn't thrilled about him marrying a Black woman. Throughout their marriage, he treated her with the same familiar behavior she had grown up with. Once again, I found myself drawn to a woman whose unresolved trauma left her incapable of receiving unconditional love. Unconsciously, we all tend to seek familiar pain until we address our own wounds.

Then, I had an epiphany. Did I truly possess the capacity for unconditional love, or was I living in a fantasy world—pretending to love in order to receive the love I desperately needed? I had never received the love of an absent father, nor the motherly love I craved after my mother's death. The core of my trauma was abandonment, and I manipulated my reality to convince myself that if I showed boundless love, women would love me in return and never leave. I now realize that my loyalty was driven by inner wounds—an unconscious reach for someone to fill the emptiness in my soul.

I continued to attract women who were unable to give themselves the unconditional love they needed, and that cycle could only be broken when I healed my inner wounds. I now know that until I nurture the wounded little child within me and learn to love myself, I will continue to attract the same pain. I am grateful for these experiences because they have set me on a path of discovery. I have come to realize that people are placed in my life not necessarily to show me who they are, but to reveal who I truly am.

CHAPTER THIRTY-TWO
A Message from The Universe

I was overwhelmed by a tidal wave of repressed memories and emotions—so much so that I found myself curled up in the fetal position, rocking back and forth in an attempt to soothe the gut-wrenching pain. I was reliving the darkest moments of my past: the terrible scenes I had suppressed for over 23 years, the warnings I had ignored, and the memories of abuse that had scarred me as a child. In that moment, I was not just battling sorrow—I was facing the demons that had haunted me since the day I witnessed my mother being doused with hot lye, the day I discovered her lifeless body, and the many times I had blamed myself for her loss.

My mind was flooded with the countless warning signs I had once ignored. I listened to her recount the brutal details of her life—her experiences in prostitution, how she preferred dealing with Caucasian men because they treated her kindly, how she had been recruited by a prostitution ring, and the degrading acts she was forced to perform. She even disclosed a horrifying incident: being taken into an abandoned house by a Black man who raped, strangled, and then threw her through a hole in the floor, leaving her for dead.

I asked myself, "What is it about me that makes me ignore all those signs?" I could only conclude that my selfish desire

Donald Smith

to get what I wanted overrode my common sense. I've come to realize that sometimes my selfishness can be both an asset and a liability. Everything that happened in my marriage wasn't really about her—it was how she coped with her own trauma.

Consistently attending NA meetings and talking about my feelings was no longer enough. I needed help outside of NA, so I decided to seek professional therapy. It took several tries to find the right therapist. I still laugh when I remember the time I scheduled an initial visit with a middle-aged Caucasian woman; during the session, I simply didn't feel that she was a good fit. I excused myself to use the restroom and never returned.

Finally, on my third attempt, I began seeing a Black female therapist who turned out to be a perfect match. She guided me through my pain, helping me realize that I had barely scratched the surface of my issues. She gave me homework assignments, and each day I wrote about my feelings. In our sessions, we methodically reviewed my writings and examined how my past trauma was causing my present pain.

She explained that traumatized people want nothing more than to feel loved and valued. Ironically, when they are truly loved and valued, they become suspicious, because it is the total opposite of what they are accustomed to. This unfamiliarity leads them to sabotage relationships by focusing on every flaw in the person offering nothing but genuine love and admiration. Conversely, when they meet someone who is abusive and neglectful—a scenario that feels all too familiar—they cling to the relationship, convincing themselves that this is the one they will love wholeheartedly. She paused and asked, "So why do you think someone who is consistently loving and caring ends up sabotaging the relationship?" I was dumbfounded; I had no answer.

She continued, "It's because the feelings of being loved and valued are uncomfortable and unfamiliar."

Listening to her describe the inner workings of a traumatized person, I saw myself in her words. I began to feel broken as she explained how our behaviors are shaped by past wounds. I told her about my experiences with my NA girl and my ex-wife, and how I ignored countless warning signs. I admitted that I pursued my desires selfishly. She gently explained that it wasn't solely my selfishness at work—it was that these relationships provided the familiar pain I had always known. In that moment, I realized that I had personalized their departure; their leaving triggered my deepest feelings of rejection and abandonment. She asked, "Surely there were women in your life who loved you unconditionally, yet you found them boring and unfulfilling?" I reluctantly agreed.

Once we identified the problem, our future sessions focused on changing my unhealthy behavior patterns. I asked, "How do I change?" She smiled and said, "You've already started the process." The journey began the moment you decided to become drug-free. It's a long, strenuous journey, but as long as you don't give up, you'll be fine. Remember, the only constant in life is change.

She suggested I read self-help literature. Although I had always relied on NA literature to guide me through difficult times, I took her advice and read books like As a Man Thinketh by James Allen, The Road Less Traveled by M. Scott Peck, and Living Through the Meantime by Iyanla Vanzant. The subtitle of the last book—"Learning to break the patterns of the past and begin the healing process"—resonated with me as if a higher power were steering me in the right direction.

She wrote about having a "basement mentality," being grounded in low self-esteem, and focusing solely on negatives while ignoring positive achievements. Ironically, I was living in the basement of my newly purchased home, even though it had three bedrooms. The metaphor was perfect for my state of mind. The next day, I gathered my mattress, box spring, and bedframe, filled my totes with clothes, and moved upstairs into the master bedroom. That seemingly insignificant move from the basement was monumental—it elevated my self-esteem.

Each day, I conscientiously worked on salvaging the broken pieces of my spirit by applying the lessons from self-help books and with the assistance of my wonderful therapist. I eventually reached a place where my newfound self-esteem made me feel good about myself and my achievements. I was still working, attending college, going to NA meetings daily, and seeing my therapist.

During one evening therapy session, I sensed something was troubling my therapist. With a heavy heart, she disclosed that her daughter had passed away from cancer. I was flabbergasted and desperate to comfort her, as she had helped me through my darkest times. In our many sessions, she had never mentioned her daughter's struggle with cancer. Of course, a good therapist keeps their personal life separate, and she was exceptional at her job.

At the end of that session, she informed me that she was taking a leave of absence and might not return. Sensing my sadness, she spent at least 30 minutes helping me process my feelings about her departure. Aware of my abandonment issues, she reassured me that her leaving had nothing to do with me. She encouraged me to continue therapy with one of her colleagues, but I refused. That day marked the last time I saw her.

CHAPTER THIRTY-THREE
On the Prowl

My job, college, Narcotics Anonymous meetings, and community business stores all became feeding grounds to quench my insatiable sexual appetite—a pursuit that mirrored my unyielding drug addiction. I used to sleep with nearly every woman in the agency on various occasions while also meeting women in the community where my job was located. Just as my drug addiction had spiraled out of control, so too had my promiscuous lifestyle become unmanageable.

I often shopped in the Timonium and Hunt Valley areas where I worked, frequently visiting Sam's Club and Rite Aid. While shopping at Sam's Club, I first noticed a beautiful cashier—a petite, vivacious woman with short hair, brown eyes, and golden-brown skin that reminded me of caramel candy. On each visit, I purposefully stood in her checkout line, no matter how long it was, just to become a familiar face. Every time I encountered her, I greeted her with warm pleasantries, eager to see her smile. After exchanging several polite greetings, I eventually revealed the true purpose behind my frequent visits: I wanted to get to know her.

We exchanged contact information and began conversing frequently over the phone. Before long, she invited me to her home. She had two children—a boy and a girl—and although we never made a verbal commitment, our behavior suggested we were a committed couple. We even went on picnics to Codorus State Park with her children and my two youngest, and I even attended her family reunion in South Hill, Virginia.

Despite these promising moments, there were frequent occasions when I attempted to initiate sex with her, only for her to deny my advances. Over time, my frustration grew, and I eventually questioned her about her sexuality. One evening, as we sat down to discuss our situation, I noticed a somber look cross her face. She began to speak about her past—a life of abuse and violence that left deep scars. She had lived in an apartment in Alexandria, Virginia, with a significant other who was brutally violent. She described incidences of physical abuse, where her body was marked with bruises, and even recounted painful episodes of violent, forced intimacy. As tears streamed down her cheeks, I realized that her trauma was still raw. I moved closer to hold and console her, but she gently pushed me away, continuing to share the horrors of her past. The thought of leaving had terrified her; she had been conditioned to believe that if she left, he would find her and kill her.

She recalled one day, while sitting outside her apartment complex, a young woman approached her and said something that made her smile. They began a casual conversation, and that newfound friend soon became a safe haven from her tumultuous relationship. Over time, they communicated secretly, and eventually, her friend revealed that she was homosexual and had fallen in love with her. At that moment, she understood that she had been groomed from the first day they met. Yet, she didn't care—no one had ever treated her with such kindness before, and she admitted to having feelings for her friend as well. The two of them eventually devised an escape plan from her abusive relationship. She left her abuser and moved into an apartment with her new lover, remaining in that relationship until about three months before we met.

When she told me her story, a heavy silence fell between us as I processed the depth of her pain. Before hearing her tale, I had been contemplating ending our relationship due to our sexual inactivity. But now I understood her reluctance to be intimate—her traumatic experiences with men had left scars that were not easily healed. Even though I knew that staying with her would be challenging, my empathy compelled me to try. She did her best to accommodate my sexual needs, though it was difficult for her—especially with oral sex, which she found particularly triggering because of her abuser's past actions. Over time, however, she managed to experience pleasure without the haunting memories

After many months, the woman I had met at Sam's Club finally found herself able to enjoy intimacy without the constant pull of her traumatic past. She had grown up in a stable, two-parent home with an older brother and had learned to value cleanliness and order—principles instilled in her by her mother, who sacrificed everything to keep her family together. Those early experiences contrasted sharply with the chaos she later endured, and as a result, she had internalized a need to cling to stability.

For about a year, we continued to see each other, but eventually, she began communicating with her ex-girlfriend, and I suspected they were rekindling an affair. When I approached her about my feelings, she adamantly denied it. Frustrated, I decided to move on.

After my time with the Sam's Club woman ended, I met another attractive, petite woman working as a Rite Aid store manager. My frequent visits to the store—for medications and photo development—turned into casual conversations, and eventually, she invited me to her home. Living alone with her teenage daughter, she appeared to be a loner who was eager for male company. Although shy at first, she gradually opened up. I took her out to one of my favorite restaurants and later invited her to my home. We talked for hours, and eventually, I lured her to my bedroom. Despite her initial tension—likely from a long period of physical abstinence—she relaxed under my kind, gentle approach.

Although she wasn't as sexually experienced as some women I had known, she was willing to follow my lead. After our intimate encounter, I took several photographs with my self-developing Polaroid camera—a habit that inflated my ego, much like notches on a gunslinger's belt. However, our time together lasted only about six months, and I soon moved on to my next adventure.

Shortly thereafter, I began seeing a woman who lived not far from college. She had three children and attended most of my classes. I resumed my familiar pattern of flirting with her, eventually leading to casual sex. When I transferred to Coppin, I discovered she was also in the social work program, and for a fleeting moment, I wondered if she was deliberately signing up for the same classes as me.

As our relationship progressed, we began including our children in each other's lives. My NA sponsor and friend, Lloyd, introduced me to the idea of vacationing outside Maryland,

and soon, our families traveled together—to Virginia Beach, Disney World, and other destinations. My friend even started a modeling program for teenagers, in which my daughter participated. We took family vacations, stayed over at each other's homes, and for a time, life felt harmonious.

Yet, as time went on, I became increasingly selfish. While my partner's modeling events occupied her weekends, I grew restless and sought out the Sam's Club girl once again. I began sneaking around between her and the model coach girl. There were nights when I would speak to the model coach on the phone, then call the Sam's Club girl for a late-night rendezvous. I would pack a bag, say good night to one, spend the night with the other, and then go to work the next morning from her home.

Eventually, I terminated my relationship with the modeling coach, but not without consequence. She cried uncontrollably and harassed me for months, forcing me to change my cell and home phone numbers. My self-centeredness left me unconcerned with her feelings; my main objective was to satisfy my own desires with my old female friend.

After living alone for a few years, I felt comfortable in my own space and made the hasty decision to allow the Sam's Club girl to move in with me. Her insecurities, however, soon overshadowed any chance at a wholesome relationship. She became clingy and accusatory. I remember inviting my siblings and friends to my birthday celebration and also inviting my children's mother, Jackie. It was winter, and my guest coats were stored upstairs. When Jackie went to retrieve her coat, I was accused of having an affair with her simply because I allowed her to go upstairs. Her insecurities became too much to bear, and after two months of tension, I asked her to leave. I felt remorseful about putting her in that position and even offered to cover her expenses as she found a new place, and she did. I even paid a friend of mine to move her into her new apartment. We have remained friends and occasionally communicate by phone.

My Sam's Club girl was determined to get married. She met a man who loved motorcycles, and she became infatuated with both him and the ride. They eventually married and now live together, sharing nothing more than their mutual passion for motorcycles.

In retrospect, the entanglements of my relationships revealed the long, tangled tentacles of addiction in every facet of my life. I sought sexual gratification as a way to numb the pain of my past, but ultimately, these relationships only deepened the void I felt inside

CHAPTER THIRTY-FOUR
Out of Control

During working hours, I would often take one of the female counselors out to visit a client, and more often than not, our visits ended at my house, where we would have sex. She was an incredibly attractive young woman, much younger than me, and we took every opportunity we could to be together. Her firm, luxurious body was a constant turn-on for me. I actually knew her mother and uncles who lived in Wilson Park when I was a teenager.

One day at work, I was trying to convince a previous sex partner to come over my house so we could spend time together. All the while, the woman I was having sex with was in the next cubicle and overheard my conversation. She later confronted me in a fit of rage, and before I knew it, a quick sharp blow came across my face. Without hesitation, I calmly walked away because I didn't want to have a physical altercation at work. I thought I had made it perfectly clear with this woman that our interactions were strictly sexual and nothing else, but I guess she didn't see it that way. She started telling other women on the job that I had a small penis, and the sex with me was awful. But yet, we had sex several times, and there were no complaints. Well, it seemed that her lies fueled the curiosity of the other women because they never disregarded my advances.

A new female employee was hired and once again I had to make my presence known. Her brown skin was unblemished, she had dreadlocks and had an Afrocentric style of dress. I introduced myself and she reciprocated by extending her hand for a handshake. In the coming days we talked and developed a cordial relationship. Our interaction remained friendly and formal until I detected a distinctive vibe coming from her body language. My mind immediately started thinking of ways for us to get together outside of the agency. We had lunch a couple of times while at work in the Timonium area where we worked.

One day we both called out from work so we could spend time together at my place. We talked about our past relationships, and how we were enjoying single life. Our first kiss was electrifying, and foreplay quickly followed. I slowly began to undress her, and she gladly assisted. The softness of her body was amazing as I began foreplay and eventually penetrating her. Approximately twenty minutes into having sex, her body was shaking violently as if she was having a seizure. But I held on like a rodeo cowboy riding a bucking horse. After a climax of sexual pleasure, we discussed the intensity of her orgasm. She explained that she never was able to obtain an orgasm during sex until that time. She further explained that in her past relationships, she always felt the need to please her man sexually without considering her own sexual needs. I asked her what made this encounter so different, she said that this time she was able to relax and allow me to take control. I don't know if she was pulling my leg or not, but I must admit that it did inflate my ego a little.

After we had been seeing each other for a while, we had a deep conversation about her past. Like several women I had known, she too had experienced horrific sexual trauma. Her first boyfriend, at the tender age of fourteen, had repeatedly raped her—with his friends sometimes joining in. She described graphic details of those early experiences, revealing that she had even volunteered to participate in the abusive acts in order to please her boyfriend. Despite the trauma, she later confided that she had been unable to achieve an orgasm until she met me.

I couldn't understand what I had done differently during our sexual encounters, but her words compelled me to search for an answer. We both explored our pasts and eventually concluded that I had validated her as a beautiful woman, allowing her to become fully engaged in our experience. This realization made me wonder how other men had treated her. She had two children and had been married before, yet her ex-husband continued to make his presence known, and on occasion, she would yield to his requests to meet.

Over time, she continued to attract men who were unkind to her. She even had a short-lived marriage to a man she barely knew. Because of her awful experiences with men, she eventually met a lesbian woman, and they married. The lesbian, however, became an alcoholic and continuously abused her mentally, physically, and emotionally. Throughout their marriage, I remained in contact with her, offering information on domestic violence and suggesting she seek therapy. Eventually, she did seek help, filed for divorce, and now lives alone with her daughter and two dogs.

In the years that followed, we stayed in touch through phone calls and occasional visits. One afternoon, while I was at work, I received a call from her, telling me that her daughter had passed away. She was devastated and wouldn't share many details about the circumstances. I knew that, prior to her daughter's death, she had lost her mother about a year before. I've come to love her as a friend, and I remain committed to being there for her in any way she needs.

I share these experiences not to inflate my ego, but to show how traumatized people attract other traumatized people into their lives. As Bryant McGill once said, "We attract what we are," and Dr. Wayne Dyer echoed, "You don't attract what you want; you attract what you are." It took me years to understand that if I changed who I was in a positive, healthy way, I would eventually attract positive, healthy people into my life.

Addiction played a major role in my insatiable appetite for sex. My drug addiction had manifested into an addiction to women—the chase, the capture, and the execution of sexual encounters became an artificial way to soothe my inner pain. I had many brief, insignificant encounters with women that are not worth mentioning, but each experience contributed to the cycle I was trapped in.

CHAPTER THIRTY-FIVE
Tragedies In the Workplace

For reasons I can't fully explain, I'd long been fascinated by mental illness and its impact on human behavior. In college, I even delivered a presentation on the commonalities among serial killers such as Jeffrey Dahmer, John Wayne Gacy, Dennis Rader (AKA BTK), and the Son of Sam, David Berkowitz—all of whom suffered from mental illnesses and had traumatic childhoods.

Working as a counselor at New Ventures—a Psychiatric Rehabilitation Program—was incredibly fulfilling for me. Despite my notorious reputation for trying to sleep with every woman I could, I excelled as a psychiatric counselor and truly loved working with my clients. The client population at New Ventures consisted mainly of adults from affluent families who funded their relatives' treatment. The agency also operated a residential program, and because I developed strong rapport with my clients, I was often assigned the most challenging cases—patients with severe mental illnesses such as schizophrenia, schizoaffective disorder, bipolar disorder, and a broad spectrum of conditions described in the DSM-5-TR.

Donald Smith

One client, a highly intelligent young man attending Purdue University, developed schizophrenia accompanied by suicidal ideations. Unable to come to terms with his mental illness, he struggled daily, and suicide became a real option for him. I frequently performed home safety inspections at his apartment to ensure a hazard-free environment. During one inspection, I discovered a loaded .38-caliber pistol hidden under his mattress. After confiscating the gun and turning it over to my administrator, I joined his treatment team for a discussion about the incident. Although he had a history of suicidal ideations, he was adamant that he would not use the gun to kill himself. Despite his convincing articulation, I remained unconvinced. The treatment team recommended a higher level of care, but before a transfer could take place, he tragically committed suicide by jumping off a bridge.

Another client on my caseload, diagnosed with schizophrenia, suffered severe episodes of auditory hallucinations. He resided with three other clients in the residential section of the program, and on many days, he would crouch in a corner, clutching his head in an effort to silence the voices—even though he was heavily medicated, the voices persisted. One of his treatment goals was to secure independent living. When an apartment became available at Tabco Towers in Towson, his treatment team arranged for him to move in, despite my strong objections that he wasn't ready. I was deeply concerned about his ability to live alone during his episodes, and I tried to visit frequently to ensure his safety. Approximately three months later, he jumped from the tenth floor, smashing into an iron dumpster. I had the urge to tell the team that I'd warned them he wasn't ready, but I kept silent, and they never acknowledged that I was right.

Years later, a young woman named Sharon Edwards from East Baltimore was hired as a counselor at New Ventures. Sharon and I developed a fantastic working relationship; I never once had any intention of pursuing her sexually. She was down-to-earth with a pleasing personality, though I noticed that when she felt disrespected, her street-smart demeanor would surface. Both staff and clients adored her, and she quickly became a significant part of our team. Every morning, our team met to review the previous day's activities and plan the day ahead. There were ample opportunities for overtime on weekends at Fordham Cottage on the campus of Sheppard Pratt—a group home for psychiatric teenage clients where the administrator often sought volunteers. I frequently worked on weekends, but one morning marked the first time Sharon volunteered for the overnight shift.

On October 9, 1995, during a morning staff meeting attended by upper management, the program director announced that on Sunday morning, October 8, 1995, Sharon had been found dead, lying in a pool of blood at Fordham Cottage. Although she had worked at New Ventures for only a year, during that time she and I had become very close friends. Despite my attempts to remain composed, I broke down in uncontrollable tears upon hearing the news. Sharon was only 27 years old and had a son. On October 13, 1995, I attended her funeral at March Funeral Home in East Baltimore.

It was later discovered that a sixteen-year-old boy, Benjamin Scott Garris, had murdered Sharon by stabbing her multiple times with a hunting knife. He escaped and was on the run for three weeks before being apprehended in Virginia Beach, Virginia. In July 1996, Benjamin Scott Garris was sentenced to life in prison without the possibility of parole plus an additional 50 years.

A woman named Patrina was then hired to replace Sharon. She moved to Baltimore from Philadelphia with her fiancé, who had secured a teaching position in Baltimore County. Although I initially tried to pursue every new woman hired, Patrina and I eventually became very good friends—I came to see her as a little sister. She played a major role in my life during my divorce from my ex-wife, and I helped her through a crisis when her fiancé cheated on her with another woman. After several years at New Ventures, she eventually moved back to Philadelphia, and we remain friends to this day.

CHAPTER THIRTY-SIX
Crossing Racial Lines

My reputation as a womanizer was well known among the staff, and for some women it only fueled their curiosity about me. One such woman was a Caucasian co-worker—a short, attractive lady whose figure was strikingly reminiscent of a Black woman's. Despite being married, she made no secret of her sexual attraction to me, and I couldn't resist her advances.

One evening, we arranged to meet at a motel. Although she appeared eager to get down to business, I wanted to understand her true intentions. I asked if she had ever had sex with a Black man before, and she admitted she hadn't. I surmised that her interest was born out of sheer curiosity—to experience what it was like to be with a Black man. Then engaged in every sexual act imaginable. I enjoyed our encounter immensely and wanted to see her again, but for weeks she avoided any contact. Finally, when we did talk, she dropped a bombshell: she was pregnant. The news hit me like a ton of bricks. At that point, I had been working at the agency for about 15 years, and I was in the process of transitioning to a job with the state of Maryland.

After leaving New Ventures, I reached out to her. She came to my new job, and we went to lunch together. Over the meal, she mentioned that she was about three months pregnant and believed the baby was her husband's. I didn't question her statement; we simply reminisced about old times at work. After that day, I didn't hear from her for nearly a year. When we finally spoke briefly over the phone, she told me she had a girl. Although I was curious about whether the baby would have blonde hair and blue eyes or Black hair and brownish skin, I didn't ask. After that conversation, she vanished from my life.

At my new job, there was a smorgasbord of women interested in me. One particular woman made a habit of coming by my office to chat—a subtle, indirect way of indicating her desire. Although she was much younger than me, I couldn't resist. We hung out a few times, and on our third meeting, we ended up in a hotel room together. The encounter, however, was disappointing: she was inexperienced and as dry as the Sahara. I tried every sexual technique I knew to help her relax, but nothing seemed to work. Sensing my dissatisfaction, she later invited me to accompany her on a home visit. After the visit, we slipped into a secluded area where she unfastened my zipper and performed oral sex on me. While her performance didn't fully excite me, I did enjoy the experience. After that encounter, we moved on, but we remained casual friends.

Working with traumatized teenagers was stressful, and one day in the agency's cafeteria I noticed a tall, beautiful, light-skinned woman with long brown hair gazing out the window like a damsel in distress. I felt compelled to approach her and offer a friendly conversation to lift her somber mood. I introduced myself, and she responded warmly with a half-smile and her name. I remarked that she looked as if she'd lost her best friend, and she admitted that the job was so stressful she wasn't sure how much longer she could cope with the unruly children. I shared my own struggles with self-care in the social work field, and she instantly seemed to relax. I could tell she was a caring and dedicated person.

Over the following days, I made it a point to stop by her office and check on her. Eventually, we began having lunch together, and I even helped her manage the challenging cases on her caseload. Our daily lunches turned into long conversations where we shared personal stories. I learned that she was unhappily married, yet she spoke of her husband as if he were her entire world—a situation that clearly stemmed from unresolved childhood trauma. I suspected she might even be adopted, given the way she described her siblings.

One afternoon, after visiting a client, we decided to have lunch in the car. During our conversation, she confided that her husband didn't know how to arouse her; their lovemaking was nothing more than a routine. Sensing an opportunity, I held her close as she poured out her frustrations. At first, she hesitated and half-heartedly pushed me away when I attempted a kiss, but eventually, her vulnerable state gave way to a passionate embrace.

After that day, I began testing my boundaries with her—gradually touching her in places a married woman shouldn't be touched. Over time, I gently fondled her until she reached orgasm, dispelling the false belief she had that she was physically incapable of pleasure. I started inviting her to have lunch at my home, my intention always to lure her into my bedroom. We shared intimate and romantic moments—dancing to her favorite love songs, laughing over small things, and engaging in deep conversations. Before long, she felt comfortable enough to step into my bedroom.

Donald Smith

As we kissed and cuddled, I could feel her body responding to my every touch. She had the body of a woman in her thirties—firm and alluring. I managed to guide her into a realm of pleasure that she had never experienced before, and for a brief moment, she basked in that newfound ecstasy. However, as I began to penetrate her, she suddenly burst into tears and jumped out of bed, declaring she couldn't continue. The reality of being intimate with another man—someone other than her husband—overwhelmed her, and the mood soured.

I tried to persuade her to continue, but instead, I held her and whispered that I understood. We got dressed and went about our day as if nothing had happened, never discussing that moment again. Eventually, she transferred to another unit within the agency, and we stopped communicating for years until we later ended up working in the same building on Howard Street. Today, we no longer speak, and I consider her the one who got away. I fell in love with her kindness and the way she treated me; if her circumstances had been different, I believe we would have made a great couple.

CHAPTER THIRTY-SEVEN
Regressed Behaviors

Attending Narcotics Anonymous meetings and seeing a therapist had once helped me find balance and make sense of the bizarre, confusing behaviors I displayed. However, during the absence of my therapist, my life began to tip off balance again. Although I still attended NA meetings, I felt abandoned, left to navigate life on my own. People in my immediate circle told me that I came across as arrogant and brusque. I convinced myself that being a nice guy never ended well in relationships—my choices always left me disappointed or heartbroken.

It eventually dawned on me that my arrogance and abrasive demeanor were attracting women. In retrospect, I now see these behaviors as a defense mechanism to protect myself from future heartbreaks and disappointments. My arrogance and abrasiveness attracted women who were searching for love in all the wrong places, and I unwittingly provided exactly what they were looking for.

I recalled a therapy session where my therapist explained that traumatized people often choose partners who are emotionally unavailable. I learned that most people have experienced some form of trauma, and that unresolved pain drives them to seek familiarity—even if that means gravitating toward selfish, emotionally unavailable, or even abusive partners. These traits, which are often associated with narcissism, reveal much about someone who is comfortable with chaos. I was once that person, unconsciously choosing such partners not once, but twice. In a desperate bid to protect myself, I even decided to become emotionally unavailable. While I'm not a narcissist, I did pack away a deeply self-centered part of myself.

I eventually became exploitative in my relationships, using women for sexual gain. My radar was always on, picking up signals from women who, like me, were searching for love in all the wrong places. No longer the "nice guy," I was on demon time.

I became a prime example of how addiction can take over other areas of life if you're not vigilant. Addiction isn't solely about drugs—it lies dormant until it finds a way to manifest in other aspects, whether through gambling, sex, alcohol, or other behaviors. I found myself reverting to my old habits.

Working with traumatized teenagers was challenging, but I loved it because they reminded me of my own troubled past. I was assigned to the most difficult cases at the agency, and when the Intensive Unit was created to address out-of-control teens, I was proud to be a part of it. Despite the hardships, I became effective at making a difference in their lives.

On several occasions, I had to visit clients in jail. My very first jail visit left me paranoid, haunted by thoughts of unsolved crimes I'd committed. Although I knew about the statute of limitations, my nerves were still frayed—until I saw my client. Ironically, he was placed in the same section

I'd been in about 35 years ago. It made me wonder if my past jail experiences were meant to prepare me to help these clients avoid a life of repeated incarcerations. After that visit, I became more comfortable with jail visits, especially since many of my teenage male clients were frequently arrested.

Although the Intensive Unit was designed for teenagers, I was once assigned to work with an eight-year-old boy and his twelve-year-old sister. The eight-year-old was sometimes more challenging than my older clients; he had a history of killing animals, stealing cars, swearing at his teachers, and even telling people to "kiss his ass." While some of my teenaged clients displayed trauma through their behavior, most of their issues were more behavioral than psychological—but they were still a handful.

I loved working with them because I saw parts of myself in their struggles. I nearly ended up in foster care when my mother passed, but my siblings fought to keep us together. I felt deeply connected to these children and understood how trauma can fuel anger, aggressive behavior, self-blame, PTSD, suicidal ideation, depression, and substance abuse. Some of my teenage clients were verbally aggressive toward me—I was cursed at, given obscene gestures, and treated rudely—but I wasn't fazed by their vulgarity because I knew it came from a place of deep hurt and trauma.

CHAPTER THIRTY-EIGHT
Black Beauty

I t was a typical day at work when I entered the lobby and noticed a woman I recognized from one of my classes at Coppin State University—Paula McCutcheon. She was the woman I had thought about long after college. Paula was small-framed with beautiful dark chocolate skin, and when she smiled, her pearly white teeth would sparkle. Although I was mesmerized by her striking Black beauty, I often hesitated to speak with her during class. She was in my last class of the evening, and my plan was always to catch her afterward—perhaps walk her to her car or offer her a ride. I assumed she wasn't taking public transportation because I would ride to the nearest bus stop, only to find that she would miraculously vanish every time, as if she had magical powers. But then, one day, she stood right in front of me, and I seized the opportunity to make my acquaintance.

We talked briefly and exchanged contact information. Eager to learn more about her, I called her every morning to say hello and strike up a conversation. One particular morning, I sensed that she was slightly irritable, speaking nonchalantly as if tired of my persistent questions. Realizing that I might be coming on too strong, I stopped calling—

and to my surprise, she called me instead. I slowed down my questioning and reassessed my approach, for something about Paula continued to spark my interest.

I told her how mesmerized I had been when I first saw her in class and how, every time after class, she seemed to disappear as if by magic. She explained that she was a single mother of three, and her main priority after class was to rush home to her children—Karla, Otis, and Gabrielle. Her words spoke volumes about her character; I could hardly imagine the sacrifices and struggles she faced to ensure her children's safety and well-being. As a child, I admired the strong Black women in my life, and Paula embodied that same resilience.

Paula worked as a social worker for a private agency, recruiting foster parents for children in care. As we grew more familiar, I would occasionally visit her at work with flowers, and we even had lunch together during working hours. Our communication became daily, and eventually we went on evening dates, with her inviting me to her home in a multi-ethnic community in Owings Mills, Baltimore County. Upon entering her impeccably clean home—a quality instilled in me by my mother, who taught that cleanliness is next to godliness—I was struck by how perfectly Paula embodied the qualities of a truly good woman. Her desirable qualities and character captured my heart.

Paula's youngest daughter lived with her, while her other two children were adults living independently. Understandably, her youngest daughter wasn't too fond of having me around; I sensed a nonchalant attitude whenever Paula introduced us. For many years, it was just Paula and her daughter, and I suspect that my presence was seen as a threat to their close bond. Despite that, Paula and I continued to see each other.

We went on dinner dates often, and one evening, as I was leaving after dinner, we shared our first electrifying kiss. Every interaction with her felt miraculous, and the more time I spent with her, the more I wanted to be near her—even though I maintained my own place, I began spending most of my time at her home.

Our first sexual encounter was very special. She allowed me to take the lead, accommodating all of my desires. If anything made her uncomfortable, she would adjust to make the experience pleasurable. She never made excuses or denied me. We practically lived together for a time, and eventually, I bought her an engagement ring and asked for her hand in marriage—and she accepted. We even took a weekend trip to Georgetown, Washington, D.C., to escape our routine. However, several months after my proposal, I became complacent, and she grew increasingly controlling.

I guess being a single mother of three for many years takes a toll—she had to manage her children's lives and dictate how they should act. That same need for control began to affect our relationship. If I did something she deemed incorrect, she wouldn't hesitate to correct me. For instance, if I slouched at a restaurant, she'd insist I sit up straight. These small corrections became increasingly annoying, and for the first time in our relationship, I began to question whether we should continue. After days of reflection, I concluded that it would be best if we remained friends.

Although our romantic relationship ended, Paula and I maintained a mutually beneficial friendship. We both knew that if one of us ever needed help, the other would be there.

The success of Paula's children is a testament to her motherly guidance and unflinching determination. I can tell how proud she is when she speaks of their accomplishments.

Her prodigy son, Otis Edward Alexander, Jr.—affectionately known as OJ—excelled in information technology, worked at Lockheed Martin at the Pentagon as an Enterprise Systems Administrator in Aberdeen, and was self-taught in Spanish and Russian. His love for music drove him to teach himself the guitar and piano while also taking aviation classes to obtain his pilot's license. He was also a self-taught photographer; he achieved an extraordinary resume by the age of thirty-four.

On Wednesday, December 14, 2017, OJ was found dead behind his home from a self-inflicted shotgun wound to the head. I remember receiving the call from Paula as if it were yesterday—I was devastated and felt profound sympathy for her and her family.

The pain of unresolved trauma can linger for years, sometimes manifesting gradually with harmful or even deadly effects, and sometimes striking in an instant—convincing people that suicide or homicide is the only permanent solution to a temporary problem. My life would have taken a very different path that night when I went to my ex-NA girl's apartment with a butcher knife. I shudder to think what might have happened if a man had been there that night—I might have ended up writing his story from a prison cell, serving a life sentence for taking another's life. But the universe and its infinite wisdom had other plans for me.

I eventually realized I was simply seeking relief from years of unresolved traumatic pain. Feeling unworthy because my mother died, my father rejected me, and both my ex-NA girl and my ex-wife left me, my abandonment issues surged with a vengeance. My common sense was overwhelmed by these issues, and I was willing to do anything to quiet my pain.

CHAPTER THIRTY-NINE
The Tentacles of Addiction

Paula was well aware of my substance abuse history, but it wasn't until after we separated that she shared her mother's story of addiction with me. She had discovered an old news documentary about heroin treatment in Baltimore City featuring her mother, Ms. Estherlene McCutcheon. When I watched the documentary, I couldn't believe how exactly Paula resembled her mother—every feature, every smile.

Ms. McCutcheon had voluntarily participated in an experimental drug treatment program for opioid addiction sponsored by the University of Baltimore. According to Dr. Isadore Tuerk from the Department of Mental Hygiene, Baltimore City ranked as the tenth most prevalent urban center for drug addicts. In a bid to find a solution, the agency launched a pilot program for treating heroin addiction at Spring Grove State Hospital. Volunteers were sorted through the Baltimore City Department of Public Welfare to take part in the project. On Wednesday, October 9, 1963, WMAR-Channel 2 broadcast a three-part television series titled The Octopus and the Addict: Law, Cure. In the opening interview, Ms. McCutcheon described addiction as an octopus—with eight appendages and rows of suckers—that held her captive.

"No matter how hard you try to escape, its vice-like grip keeps you in captivity," she said.

Her words struck a deep chord with me. I could clearly relate to her octopus analogy; I, too, was ensnared by the obsessive, compulsive need to get and use drugs, doing whatever it took to satisfy both physical and mental cravings. That vicious cycle—stealing from family, robbing people, shoplifting—repeated for days, weeks, and even years, until eventually I became so sick and tired of being sick and tired that I finally sought help.

Ms. McCutcheon also spoke about the stigma associated with drug addiction—how society and law enforcement dehumanize addicts, treating them as monsters. "Heroin addicts are just like alcoholics who can seek treatment, but heroin addicts are basically on their own," she pleaded. Her motivation for detoxing was simple: she wanted a new life for herself and her three children. After numerous unsuccessful attempts to quit on her own, she suspected that her addiction might have stemmed from a traumatic childhood experience. She vividly recalled the first time she smoked marijuana at age twelve, and how that eventually led her to heroin.

In 1956, she was twice placed on probation for shoplifting. Then, in 1960, she was arrested again and sentenced to three years at the Maryland Reformatory for Women (now known as the Maryland Institution for Women). At the time, her three children were placed in the foster care system. While incarcerated, Ms. McCutcheon endured a harrowing six-day heroin withdrawal in her prison cell—worse, she described, than childbirth, with excruciating nerve pain, muscle cramps, profuse sweating, and loss of bowel control.

Maryland's three-strike mandatory sentence law meant that if she was caught shoplifting again, she'd face life imprisonment without parole—a terrifying prospect that drove her to seek help through the Baltimore City Department of Public Welfare. The documentary showed footage of Ms. McCutcheon kissing her children goodbye as she left with her social worker, Ms. Doris Polston, with her children—young Paula and her two sisters—waving goodbye. Ms. McCutcheon was then transported to Springfield State Hospital for treatment.

Before 1987, the medical community regarded heroin addiction as a mental health disorder rather than a disease, a classification that changed only later with the AMA's recognition of addiction as a disease. For years, Black and Brown communities have been saturated with heroin, cocaine, crack, fentanyl, and now guns—a direct correlation between drug abuse, crime, and the explosive rate of incarcerations among these populations. Based on my own observations and experiences, it appears that local and federal governments only began seeking solutions when white suburban children became alarmingly addicted. Conspiracy theories even suggest that drugs and guns were intentionally introduced into Black and Brown communities to systematically destroy these races—a subject for another book.

Ms. McCutcheon described the daily choices heroin addicts made to secure their next fix, using street slang to detail activities like "hanging paper" (forgery), "boosting" (shoplifting), "playing the murphy" (con games), and prostitution. Her primary hustle was shoplifting. The experimental treatment at Springfield was based on untested ideas and techniques that were still in their infancy. According to the documentary The Octopus and the Addict: Law, Cure, in 1963 there were only

Donald Smith

two facilities in the United States treating opium addiction—
operated by the Federal Public Health Services in Fort Worth,
Texas, and Lexington, Kentucky. Dr. Tuerk noted that "90%
of the people who completed the programs at Lexington,
Kentucky, and Fort Worth, Texas, were back using drugs
within six months," a dismal success rate attributed to the
lack of follow-up housing and job opportunities for patients
after their release. It was said that Billie Holiday had been
sentenced to the Lexington facility for opium treatment. In
1974, the Federal Bureau of Prisons took over the Lexington
facility and converted it into a coed federal prison—a facility
I, too, would later know from my seven-and-a-half-year stint
for bank robbery.

The challenges of treating opium addiction left the
facilitators and physicians scrambling for effective
interventions to manage Ms. McCutcheon's acute
withdrawals. They administered medications to ease her
pain for the first 48 hours, then discontinued them, deeming
the period sufficient—an assumption that proved tragically
inadequate. Ms. McCutcheon continued to suffer withdrawal
symptoms, and despite her pleas for additional relief, she was
denied medication. Days later, she opted out of the program
and returned home to her children—a move that surprised
everyone involved, as she had appeared enthusiastic and
determined to achieve sobriety. I couldn't tell if the facilitators
and physicians were genuinely concerned for her well-being
or if they simply viewed her as a research project. However, I
could sense the sincerity and diligence of her social worker,
Ms. Polston, whose commitment to Ms. McCutcheon's
recovery was evident.

Ms. McCutcheon was in her mid-twenties, caring for
three children and an aunt with physical disabilities. Sadly,

she returned to the same challenging conditions and social environment she had left before seeking treatment. Although she managed to stay drug-free for a while, her limited understanding of addiction eventually led her back into its grasp. She used drugs intermittently for years until she passed away in her fifties from a chronic blood disorder. I believe she would have been proud to know that her three children grew up to be productive members of society, each a testament to her strength. Against all odds, her children persevered through their trauma—Paula worked for the Department of Public Safety and Correctional Services, later earning a master's in social work and now enjoying retirement as a grandmother; her oldest sister became an attorney; and her younger sister, following in their mother's footsteps, eventually achieved sobriety and a productive life.

CHAPTER FORTY
Positive Influence

The foster care system is largely staffed by women from all walks of life, many of whom are drawn to the field by an innate desire to help others. Often, this need to help stems from their own unresolved trauma. Trauma can manifest in a multitude of ways—some destructive, some healing. For many, channeling their pain into helping others is a form of self-therapy, a way to find purpose in the chaos of their past.

For me, the struggles of addiction and the scars of trauma ignited a passion to guide others toward healing. I found my calling in working with teenagers in the foster care system, many of whom had experienced neglect, abandonment, and abuse. Helping them work through their trauma became my purpose. For the first time in my life, I wasn't focused solely on myself. While not every child on my caseload thrived—some ended up in prison—many overcame their circumstances and became successful, productive adults.

During my time as a caseworker, I met a social worker who shared my passion for working with foster youth. One of my teenage girls had been placed in an independent living program, and we both played a role in ensuring her success.

From the start, I admired this woman's dedication to her job. She was meticulous, professional, and had a no-nonsense approach to her work. While she was warm and personable, she never veered off course when it came to her clients.

Unlike most women I encountered, she didn't seem the least bit interested in me romantically, which only piqued my curiosity. By this point, I considered myself a ladies' man, someone who could easily read a woman's attraction. But with her, I got nothing—no signals, no lingering eye contact, no flirtation. That only made me more determined to get to know her.

As we continued working together, I learned we were both enrolled in the Master of Social Work program at Morgan State University. However, I was a year ahead of her. She happened to be in classes with two women I had previously been involved with. One night, during a class discussion, the topic of phone contacts came up, and these two women started bickering over who had my cell and home number. She later told me she was shocked by their pettiness, but I couldn't tell whether the situation intrigued her or turned her off.

Eventually, my persistence paid off, and we went out for lunch. Our conversation was easy, flowing from work to school to our mutual choice to be pescatarians. After that first lunch, we began speaking on the phone daily and occasionally meeting up in person.

During this time, I planned to attend a Narcotics Anonymous convention in Philadelphia with a few friends. We spoke on the phone almost the entire trip. Up to that point, I hadn't disclosed my history as a recovering addict. I simply told her I was traveling with some male friends. That night, while still on the phone, she abruptly asked me if I was gay. I laughed and explained that I was in NA, and the trip was for a convention. I assumed her question stemmed from her confusion about why a grown man would voluntarily take a trip with other men. That conversation made me realize that my persistence was working—she was thinking about me in a deeper way.

In 2008, I graduated from Morgan, and she finished her program the following year. Over time, we became close friends. The more I got to know her, the more I realized I wanted her in my life in a significant way. We both valued health and wellness and often went on walks around Lake Montebello and through the wooded trails of Montebello Park.

One thing that stood out to me was how rigid she was about following rules. Around the lake, arrows were painted on the pavement to direct pedestrian traffic, and she was adamant about only walking in the designated direction. To me, this was insignificant, but for her, rules existed for a reason.

At first, I dismissed it, but later, I recognized the lesson in it. All my life, I had lived by my own rules, breaking societal norms and bending moral boundaries to suit my desires. Even in recovery, I still struggled with selfishness and entitlement. She, on the other hand, had a disciplined, structured way of approaching life. Her steadfastness in following even the smallest rules made me reflect on how much I had resisted structure. Without knowing it, she was showing me a different way to live—one with integrity and self-discipline.

She also held me accountable in ways no other woman had. She refused to accept my nonsense or make excuses for me. At first, I found it frustrating, but over time, I realized how much I respected her for it. Most women I had dated accepted me as I was, no questions asked. If they had a problem with my behavior, I simply moved on. But she was different. She challenged me to be better, and I admired that about her.

Though I was eighteen years her senior, she had an old soul. Unlike many women her age, she wasn't scattered or indecisive—she was laser-focused on what she wanted in life. And at that time, she made it clear that a relationship wasn't one of those things.

I still remember the day at Lake Montebello when I asked her to be my woman. Without hesitation, she said no. My ego took a major hit. I had never been rejected like that before, but instead of walking away, I became even more determined.

Despite her refusal, she began sending me mixed signals. She treated me like her man in every way except for the physical aspects of a relationship. She knew what I needed before I even voiced it. She was always there for me, making sure I was taken care of. Although she insisted she didn't want a relationship, her actions told a different story.

At first, I found it confusing, but as I got to know her past, it all made sense. She had been deeply hurt in previous relationships. Every man she had been with had cheated on her, and that betrayal left scars. I realized that acting like a girlfriend—but not actually committing—was her defense mechanism. She wanted the bond and connection but was terrified of being hurt again.

Even introducing me to her son and immediate family took time. It was over a year before she felt comfortable enough to let me into that part of her world. Looking back, I see that she needed time to trust that I wasn't a threat to her well-being.

Through her, I learned patience. I learned discipline. And, for the first time, I understood what it meant to truly earn someone's trust.

CHAPTER FORTY-ONE
Family Dynamics

Family dynamics profoundly shape a person's development, behavior, and character throughout life. The interactions we have with our parents during childhood play a crucial role in how we relate to others—especially with members of the opposite sex. In her case, she was raised in a two-parent household where, for generations, women were the primary caretakers. Her father, though a good provider with a well-paid job, eventually succumbed to his inner demons, turning to drugs and extramarital affairs. As a result, family, work, and household responsibilities took a backseat to his addiction and street life. The allure of the street and the lure of relationships can be as addictive as drugs, providing a false sense of security and validation for those suffering from unresolved trauma.

I am unaware of the details of her father's upbringing, but his story likely mirrors that of thousands of others caught in the grip of drugs, sex, and the lifestyle of the streets—a reality that afflicted countless Black families during the '70s and '80s, including both our families. While many members of her family, aside from her grandmother, mother, and herself, struggled with addiction, she grew up surrounded by relatives addicted to alcohol, drugs, and the street life. One of her uncles even lived an extravagant lifestyle as a drug dealer. From an early age, she developed a deep disdain for addicts and the street lifestyles of drug dealers, hustlers, and pimps.

It was this background that made it all the more significant when she eventually accepted someone like me into her life. I had lived the street lifestyle and embodied many of the things she had come to despise. Yet, because I had escaped the grip of drugs and the streets, she saw me as a symbol of hope—a man who had broken free and become a productive member of society. According to her, I was the first person she had ever met who had managed to escape addiction and rebuild their life.

The complexities of addiction and the factors that lead so many Black families into substance abuse—environment, trauma, and self-worth—are vast. I suspect that addiction may even have hereditary components, with the traits of an addicted parent passed down to their children. Could this be why so many Black families have been plagued by addiction for generations?

Her relationship with her father was virtually non-existent. She described him as having a nasty disposition—angry most of the time—and she felt physically ill whenever he came home. Raised by her mother, she was given strict instructions to care for her father's needs, like preparing his meals, as well as looking after her brothers. I recall her explaining that her father would sometimes ride past her at the bus stop, and I told her he was probably on a mission to get drugs—a testament to the tunnel vision of addiction.

Fragmented Memories of a Man Child

Growing up in a neighborhood filled mostly with single-parent households, she had no positive examples of a father-daughter relationship. Her lack of a bond with her father influenced her views on what a healthy relationship should be, and it inevitably affected her future relationships with men. She had no desire to seek her father's love and affection; his absence became her accepted reality. There were days when she dreaded seeing him come home. Her relationships with her brothers and uncles were similarly one-sided, as she was taught to care for them without receiving the same care in return.

In stark contrast, her mother was a strong woman with an unwavering commitment to her family—the nicest woman I have ever met. Her determination to keep the family together often meant overlooking the misbehavior of her husband and children. Growing up in an era when women were expected to take care of their men no matter the circumstances, she passed on that philosophy to her daughter, teaching her to care for a man in a relationship.

I firmly believe that the law of attraction brought us together. "You don't attract what you want; you attract who you are." I was a man controlled by the needs of my inner child—the child who longed to be cared for like a daughter by his mother. I believe her inner child, in turn, longed for the love and attention of her absent father. It is no coincidence that she attracted a man who shared characteristics with her father. Both her father and I were the youngest male children in our families, spoiled by female siblings and relatives. We both have a long history of drug abuse and self-centeredness, and our birthdays are just two days apart. The only difference is that I have been in recovery for 35 years and have made miraculous changes in my life, while he continues to struggle with active addiction.

As we continued to see each other, I grew frustrated that she treated me like I was her man but wouldn't commit to an actual relationship. I did everything in my power to ensure that she wouldn't slip away—I became relentless in my pursuit, and eventually, she accepted me as her partner.

I remember our first sexual encounter vividly. My long-suppressed desire for her finally surfaced, but during the warm-up, I sensed an awkwardness in her attempts at affection. She seemed tense and unable to relax, as if preoccupied with the impending encounter. Her discomfort forced me to take control, and I became overly aggressive. Later, she explained that my aggressiveness had diminished her enjoyment. I realized it was difficult for her to simply relax and savor the moment.

Over time, I began to see how her absent father affected her ability to be intimate with men. I recall an incident when she saw my daughter sitting on my lap, and later she told me that she found it inappropriate. My daughter and I shared a close father-daughter relationship—a bond she had never experienced. I believe that intimacy is learned through early family interactions. Although my mother never said "I love you," I felt her love through her care, occasional hugs, and the sparkle in her eyes. In contrast, she was never shown affection; her father was absent, and her mother taught her to be a caretaker from the age of thirteen, often neglecting the nurturing that fosters intimacy.

She mastered caregiving to the point where she tended to others' needs while neglecting her own. One of the qualities that attracted me to her was her instinctive ability to care for me, often before I even realized I needed it. She kept my inner child happy and filled the void left by the absence of the nurturing love I had longed for in my own life.

I realized that I had a pattern of subconsciously seeking out women with caregiving qualities—qualities reminiscent of my mother. Her absence left a deep void in my life, and until I healed my inner wounds, I continued to attract women unable to give unconditional love. I now understand that this cycle can only be broken once I learn to heal my inner child. Only then will I attract love, peace, honesty, and loyalty from others. I am grateful for this experience, for it has set me on a path of discovery. I now realize that people come into my life not to show me who they are, but to reveal who I truly am.

CHAPTER FORTY-TWO
Two wounded Souls

I believe relationships are designed to expose what is missing inside of us, to force us to reflect and confront the wounds we have yet to heal. As I reflect on my own journey, I realize that once again, I have allowed my wants to blind me to warning signs in a woman—signs that, if acknowledged, could have saved me from a great deal of pain.

It has been years since my partner and I have had sexual intimacy, and any form of true closeness between us has been non-existent. Yet, I had continued to hold on to the way she treated and cared for me. I had plenty of opportunities to be with other women, but I chose not to. I flirted occasionally, but I never crossed the line into infidelity.

This time, however, my inability to heed the warning signs led me to a deeper level of self-discovery. I have come to understand that relationships serve as mirrors, reflecting the unresolved wounds that require our attention. That 15-year relationship had brought me to the painful conclusion that my inner child's trauma had only been pacified, not healed.

My partner fulfilled my need for a woman who cared for me the way my mother once did, soothing the restless longing

I've carried since childhood. But there was no real healing—only temporary relief. If she were to leave, that same need would resurface, and the cycle would continue. I would find myself searching for yet another woman to fulfill the role that I've unconsciously assigned to every significant relationship in my life.

Over the years, our relationship had become increasingly challenging for both of us. It had forced me to take a deeper dive into my own inner self. I must reach a place where I am no longer searching for my mother's love in other women to feel whole. The love I seek must be found within myself.

The catalyst for this realization came when my relationship came to an abrupt end. She told me she could no longer continue because I was unable to meet her emotional needs in the way she required. What she didn't realize was that her longing for emotional care stemmed from the absence of emotional connection from the significant men in her life—her father, her uncles, and her brothers.

If the wound inflicted by her father remains unhealed, she will continue to end up with men who cannot provide the emotional stability she desperately seeks. The truth is, we were both searching for something we hadn't yet been able to give ourselves. Our unhealed wounds began manifesting as arguments, insecurities, and the belief that leaving the relationship would ease the pain.

She would often be moved to tears when she felt neglected by me, convinced that I was failing her. She concluded that she could no longer stay. But she was blind to the real origin of her need—the lack of love and affection she didn't receive from her father. Though she consciously believed that his absence hadn't affected her, subconsciously, it planted a seed—one that grew into a deep craving to be cared for.

The woman who had taken care of my emotional needs was now walking away, triggering my deepest abandonment fears. I tried everything I could to convince her to stay. Once again, I was left feeling as if I wasn't good enough, as if someone who played a significant role in my life no longer wanted me. My inner child—the one who had briefly found joy and comfort—began to weep.

I begged her not to end things. I tried every way I knew to make her stay, but nothing I did was ever enough. The harder I tried to please her, the more apparent it became that I was trying to become the man she wanted, rather than the man I needed to be for my own healing.

I had concluded that I was trying to change into the man that she wanted me to be instead of the man that I needed to be for my own healing. I also knew her history with a man who worshiped the ground she walked on, and he provided anything her heart desired. Although she said he was a little eccentric, he treated her like a queen. And yet she labeled him as a stalker and being too preoccupied with making her happy. The feelings of being cared for in this manner overwhelmed her, and she discontinued her relationship with him, and at some point, she stopped communicating with him all together.

This scenario appears to be similar to my NA-girl and x-wife and how people can become comfortable with familiar pain. My significant other chose to be in a relationship with a man who had characteristic traits like her father and was unable to provide her with what she needed emotionally. After 15 years of being a caregiver, she has come to a place where she felt depleted and resentful because I wasn't able to pour back into her emotionally like she was able to do for me. There's a little boy and a little girl inside of us that are still stuck, crying out for the unmet needs from childhood. We expect the closest people around us to fulfill that need, but that need never gets fulfilled from the outside (awakeningwithbrian).

I believe that we all have an automatic physiological reaction to an event that is perceived as stressful or frightening. This built-in mechanism causes us to adjust to our unpleasant situations in ways that can be healthy or unhealthy. Most of the time we choose the latter. In my situation, the way I coped with my childhood trauma and inner pain was to use drugs. The way my significant other dealt will her trauma was to become a caregiver to the very people who neglected to care for her emotionally as a child. She is not only a caregiver towards me, but also a caregiver towards everyone who has a place in her life. She has an incredible talent for caring for others and solving their problems, but she doesn't have a clue about how to take care of herself. As a child she learned that to receive love, she had to put her own needs aside. So, she thinks to love someone she must sacrifice her own needs.

I surmise that this was her coping mechanism as a child, she cared for her father, uncles, and brothers who were incapable of reciprocating the love, attention, and security she needed as a child. Her quest for helping others overshadows her desires to feel validated by those she loves, and therefore the absence of feeling loved, and affection continues to drive her need to satisfy others.

We had hard conversations about the condition of our relationship, and I was the one that was mostly blamed because I wasn't able to take care of her in the way that she needed me to. The only responsibility she owned was that she enabled me for 15 years to be the man I was. I was able to recognize my self-centeredness, and I worked on change, but my efforts weren't good enough for her. I finally became frustrated, and with frustration, I decided not to fight for the continuation of our relationship. Besides, a relationship is doomed to fail if your partner focuses on your issues and refuses to see their own.

My childhood trauma continuously dictated my behavior to seek the love of my mother that has been gone since the day she died over fifty years ago. So, all those years I have searched outside of myself to find ways to appease the needs of my inner child. But if I wish to end this vicious cycle, I must focus on healing my unmet childhood needs through the process of forgiveness and self-love. The truth is that I can learn to give myself the very needs that I know are missing in my life, and it will allow me to feel whole.

On the other hand, what if my feelings of brokenness are all an illusion that was created by my childhood trauma? What if there's nothing to fix, and everything I think I need I already possess? What if my abandonment issues are all an illusion to help me make sense of the absence of my father and the death of my mother? If in fact those feelings are illusions, the conjured feelings that felt real, and sent me on a path of self-destruction. So, my job is to figure out the answers to those questions. Do I really possess all that I need to become whole, and if so, how do I tap into it? This is definitely a difficult conundrum.

CHAPTER FORTY-THREE
My Children

My concept of family was instilled in me from childhood, when I always saw strong women as the head of the household. My father, grandfather, and the fathers of my siblings were all absent, so the importance of being a father didn't resonate with me until much later in life. I don't want to sugarcoat or justify my actions for being a terrible father to some of my children. I never really understood the value of a father–son relationship because of the environment in which I was raised. I was oblivious to the impact that an absent father would have on a young boy until I eventually conducted a searching moral inventory of my life.

I discovered that I carried a father wound that subconsciously influenced my behavior and my negative thoughts about myself throughout my teenage and young adult years. My feelings of not being good enough stemmed from the absence of my father, and my mother's death only exacerbated those feelings. I carried this low self-worth into adulthood, lacking the guidance of a strong father and the nurturing presence of a loving mother. I had no idea what was happening inside me until I reached a point where I no longer wanted to feel worthless, and I decided to work on myself. Unknowingly, I passed on these same negative feelings to my sons by failing to be a strong, positive presence in their lives. My greatest contributions to this life are my children: Kevin, Dana, Lakeisha, Janiqua, James, and Daris.

Earlier in my life, several factors hindered my ability to be a father to three of my sons. I became a father at the age of 14 when Kevin was born, and our father–son relationship was virtually nonexistent. I was too caught up in drugs and the street lifestyle; my only concerns were obtaining drugs and satisfying my own selfish needs. Frequent incarcerations kept me away from my children for years at a time, and I am grateful for their mothers and grandparents who raised them in a loving and caring environment. My own contributions to their lives were limited to choosing partners who lived a lifestyle opposite of my own. Although two of those women later fell victim to the drug life, they were truly good women.

Kevin was well cared for by his mother's family, and although we were in each other's presence occasionally, I never knew how to interact with him properly. Feelings of awkwardness and discomfort led me to justify having less frequent contact. I could see, even at a young age, that he enjoyed being in my company, but my selfishness always compelled me to prioritize my own needs over being a present father.

When Kevin's grandmother passed away, he ended up moving into a dysfunctional household with his mother, Yvonne, and her boyfriend Gary—yes, the same Gary I had befriended during my time in Federal prison. Yvonne gave birth to three other children with Gary, and they all lived together on Greenmount Avenue, along with Kevin and my daughter LaKeisha. By that time, both Yvonne and Gary were heavy drug users, and both were infected with AIDS. I recall visiting their home in early recovery; no one was there except Gary, who was in the midst of drawing heroin into a syringe. Knowing I was in recovery, he offered to share his heroin with me. Although the addict in me wanted to accept, the recovering side respectfully declined, and I left immediately.

Domestic violence was a frequent occurrence between Gary and Yvonne, and there were many occasions when Kevin clashed with Gary, as he tried to protect his mother. I often heard terrible things happening in their household. When my daughter LaKeisha's safety became a concern, I moved her in with me and my NA girlfriend. Eventually, Kevin had enough of the chaos and chose to live with his aunt Marian (also known as Jahara). Later, he moved in with his uncle Rodney and his wife. I eventually learned that Kevin needed a stable place to stay, so I contacted a friend whose stepson ran a boardinghouse, and a room was made available for him. I assisted in his move, and it has been 15 years or more since I have seen my son. I was curious to know how he felt about my absence, so we had a long conversation about our lives. He forgave me for not being the father he deserved, but I could still see the little boy within him who longed for his father's attention; he, too, had become a man-child.

Kevin shared that he married a Caucasian woman at a young age and has two sons who are now grown men. I don't know much about his relationship with his children, but I suspect that my absence played a significant role in their dynamic. Kevin also committed adultery and had a third son with another Caucasian woman—I have yet to meet my grandsons. Each interaction with him revealed a lack of the growth and stability needed for self-sufficiency. We have had numerous conversations about the importance of managing his finances and self-care, but it seems our talks have yielded little change. I once thought my absence was the primary cause of his struggles, and I tried to make up for the past by helping him as much as I could. Eventually, I had to accept his reality—true change can only come from within.

I was just 15 when my son Dana was born, and I was never a proper father figure to him. His mother, uncles, and grandparents raised him to be an outstanding young man. Although his mother sometimes arranged visits between Dana and me, I still felt awkward around him, partly because I was a 16-year-old drug addict and criminal, focused solely on getting and using heroin at the time.

Dana developed a passion for breakdancing and rap music, talents that led him to the Baltimore School of the Arts in tenth grade, where he befriended Tupac Shakur. Tupac lived at 3955 Greenmount Avenue in East Baltimore, and they spent considerable time together. Eventually, Dana moved to California to join Tupac, and I received updates from his mother. In 1992, when I had two years of sobriety, I learned that Dana had appeared in Tupac's video "Brenda's Got a Baby." I immediately searched on YouTube and, to my immense pride, saw him living his dream as a rap artist. He went on to appear in several more Tupac videos, but his career with Tupac was short-lived once Tupac became involved with unsavory characters in the music industry. Eventually, Dana returned to Baltimore.

While I was in recovery and working hard to become a better man and father, I was determined to make up for my past failures. I used every resource available to locate Dana. I eventually discovered he was working at a restaurant in

Towson. The thought of him potentially rejecting me filled me with nervousness, but I mustered the courage to visit him. One afternoon, I showed up at his job and waited in a booth until he arrived. We sat on opposite sides of a table, and I could instantly sense his resentment toward me. Although he seemed unconcerned with my presence, I initiated a conversation about my long absence. I realized his reaction came from deep hurt, and I understood his feelings, even though I couldn't immediately alleviate them. All I could do was continue reaching out in hopes that one day he would forgive me.

After that meeting, we attempted to maintain contact, but his unhealed wounds eventually caused him to disconnect. Over the years, I received occasional pictures and updates from his mother, including memories of him working with Tupac. I am an avid viewer of the TV show Unsung, and one day I watched a segment on Tupac in which Dana appeared discussing his experiences. That moment stirred a mix of pride, regret, and guilt about our father–son relationship. Compelled by these emotions, I reached out once more in hopes of forging a deeper bond, but his inability to let go of the past kept him stuck in resentment. Some people live a lifetime without healing their childhood wounds, and I ultimately had to respect his decision not to have a relationship with me.

My relationship with my daughters and youngest son was different from my relationships with my oldest boys. Although I was in active addiction, my daughter LaKeisha always lived with me and her mother. Amid the chaos of drug use and criminal activities, LaKeisha captured my heart. She was my little angel, and I always took care of her, even during my darkest times. Every time I returned from arrest or prison, she was there with open arms.

Donald Smith

When I came home from federal prison, LaKeisha was living with her mother and Gary in an unhealthy environment—both using drugs, with Gary being extremely abusive. At the time, she was a teenager, struggling under those conditions. I had been in recovery for about three years and had my own apartment with my NA girlfriend, so when I learned of her situation, I invited her to live with me. My NA girlfriend wasn't happy about the decision, but since the apartment was in my name, I made the choice for her safety. Soon after moving in, I discovered that LaKeisha was pregnant. My granddaughter was born prematurely and required a feeding tube until she could eat on her own.

Due to my NA girlfriend's increasingly negative behavior and our relationship problems, we eventually broke up, and she moved out. Approximately one year later, I met my ex-wife and left the apartment to my daughter. LaKeisha proved to be remarkably responsible—she kept a job, paid bills on time, and eventually moved out on her own, went to college, and graduated with a degree in nursing. Both her mother and Gary later passed away from complications related to AIDS. On August 30, 2002, I attended Yvonne's funeral at March Funeral Home.

While raising her own two children, LaKeisha took on the responsibility of caring for her three siblings. Today, they are all adults living independently. My two granddaughters, Taneira and Kayla, are thriving—Taneira is a Baltimore City police officer, and Kayla runs her own hair styling business in Atlanta, Georgia. I am very proud of their accomplishments, and I maintain a wonderful relationship with her mother's three other children—Danielle, Devon, and Corey—who are also living successful lives.

My daughter Janiqua has always been a constant presence in my life. I witnessed her birth in 1991 when I had just one year of sobriety in NA. There were times when I watched her while I was unemployed, and her mother had to work to support the family. Although I remained a steady father figure in her life, I also engaged in relationships with other women. I once impregnated a woman named Tonya, who gave birth to my son James. Despite living drug-free, I struggled to navigate life's challenges. My drug addiction had morphed into an addiction to women.

My father–daughter bond with Janiqua became unbreakable; she became daddy's little girl. I would go jogging and do floor exercises at home, and she would join me, mimicking my movements even at the age of three. I have been a consistent father throughout her life. Now an adult, she works as a lieutenant with the Baltimore City Fire Department. We share a close relationship, and I am immensely proud of her. She is also a divorced mother of two beautiful children, Chance and Cannyn, who affectionately call me "Grandy."

My son James and I never quite established a true father–son relationship. As I mentioned earlier, James was conceived while I was living with Jackie, although I also saw his mother. I was in active addiction when he was born, but I entered recovery when he was three years old. I didn't become actively involved in his life until he was about 10 or 11. I made an effort to have him spend time with Janiqua and Daris so that they could form a bond, all while I struggled to figure out this new way of fatherhood. Eventually, however, my relationship with James became superficial and lacked the depth a father and son should share. Our interactions became transactional; I would hear from him only when he needed something. One day, during a phone conversation, I asked if our relationship was solely based on what I could do for him, and he admitted that it was. I was still in early recovery and too immature to handle his hurtful response, so instead of addressing the issue, I eventually cut ties completely. I rationalized that he would be better off with his mother and her husband.

I met his stepfather—a church-going man who seemed to be a positive role model for James. His mother never interfered with our relationship; whenever he brought up our issues, she would simply say, "That's between you and your father. You two can work it out." Seventeen years passed before I finally reached out to James in an attempt to establish a relationship. He and Janiqua would occasionally communicate on social media, so I asked her to request his phone number. When I finally called, he wouldn't answer, so I left a message. Later, he texted back, asking why I was reaching out after all these years. I explained that I wanted to get to know him better and hoped to build a relationship. He replied that he preferred texting and that, as a stranger, my return wouldn't enhance his life. He said the only thing he was interested in was getting to know his siblings. Despite his insistence that my absence had no effect on his life, I could hear the hurt and resentment in every word. We continued to communicate by text from January 9, 2023, to December 22, 2023. I discovered that he was an intelligent yet introverted young man, a talented rapper, and a gifted writer. Although we talked about our lives, our conversations never reached the level needed to heal his resentment. I repeatedly asked if we could meet in person, but he always declined. On his birthday, December 21, 2023, I invited him to celebrate, and he said he was busy. The following day, I sent him a text— and have yet to receive a reply.

In contrast, my relationship with my daughters and my youngest son was very different from that with my older boys. Although I was in active addiction, my daughter LaKeisha always lived with me and her mother. Even in the midst of drug use and criminal activity, LaKeisha was my little angel, and I always made sure she was cared for. Every time I returned from jail or prison, she greeted me with open arms.

When I came home from federal prison, LaKeisha was living with her mother and Gary in an unhealthy environment. Yvonne and Gary were both using drugs, and Gary was very abusive. At that time, LaKeisha was a teenager, and her difficulties with Gary's inappropriate behavior became too much. After I had been in recovery for about three years and had my own apartment with my girlfriend, I invited LaKeisha to live with me. My NA girlfriend wasn't thrilled about my decision, but since the apartment was in my name, I made the choice for her safety. Shortly after LaKeisha moved in, I discovered she was pregnant. My granddaughter was born prematurely and had to be fed through a feeding tube until she could eat on her own.

Later, my NA girlfriend's attitude deteriorated, and our relationship eventually ended; she moved out. Approximately one year later, I met my ex-wife and left the apartment to LaKeisha. She proved remarkably responsible—keeping a job, paying bills on time—and eventually moved out on her own, went to college, and graduated with a nursing degree. Both her mother and Gary later passed away from complications of AIDS. On August 30, 2002, I attended Yvonne's funeral at March Funeral Home.

While raising her own two children, LaKeisha took on the responsibility of caring for her three siblings, and all are now adults living independently. My two granddaughters,

Taneira and Kayla, are thriving—Taneira is a Baltimore City police officer, and Kayla runs her own business as a hairstylist in Atlanta, Georgia. I am incredibly proud of their accomplishments, and I also maintain a wonderful relationship with her mother's three other children: Danielle, Devon, and Corey, who are all living successful lives.

My daughter Janiqua has always been present in my life—I witnessed her birth in 1991, just one year into my sobriety with NA. Even when I was unemployed and her mother had to work to support the family, I remained a constant father figure, despite my own flaws and my involvement with other women. I once impregnated a woman named Tonya, who gave birth to my son James. Although I was living drug-free, I struggled to adapt to life's challenges. My drug addiction had morphed into an addiction to women.

My bond with Janiqua grew unbreakable—she became daddy's little girl. I would go jogging, and after returning home, we'd do exercises together. She was around three years old at the time, and I have been a consistent presence in her life ever since. Now an adult, she works as a lieutenant with the Baltimore City Fire Department. We share a close relationship, and I am immensely proud of her. She is also a divorced mother of two beautiful children, Chance and Cannyn, who affectionately call me "Grandy."

My relationship with my son James never developed into a true father–son bond. As I mentioned earlier, James was conceived while I was living with Jackie, though I also saw his mother. I was in active addiction when he was born, and although I entered recovery when he was three, I didn't become actively involved in his life until he was around 10 or 11. I tried to bring him together with Janiqua and Daris, hoping they would form a bond, all while I struggled with the demands of newfound fatherhood. Eventually, my relationship with James became superficial—he would only reach out when he needed something. One day, during a phone conversation, I asked if our relationship was solely transactional, and he admitted that it was. Still in early recovery and too immature to handle his hurtful response, I eventually cut ties with him, justifying my decision by thinking he'd be better cared for by his mother and her husband. I met his stepfather—a church-going man who appeared to be a good role model for James—and my daughter's mother would simply say, "That's between you and your father. You two can work it out." Seventeen years passed before I reached out to James in an attempt to establish a relationship. Though we communicated on social media for a time, our conversations never seemed to heal his resentments. I invited him to dinner several times, but he always declined. On his birthday in December 2023, I reached out again, only to receive no response.

Though my relationship with my older sons was fraught with missed opportunities and deep regrets, my bond with my daughters and my youngest son was different. Despite my struggles with addiction, my daughter LaKeisha always remained my little angel. I was there for her even during my darkest times, and every time I returned from prison, she welcomed me with open arms.

I am truly blessed to have each of my children in my life. They have grown into responsible, productive members of society, and I am a proud father.

CHAPTER FORTY-FOUR
Significate Losses: The Generational Curse

There are three inevitable outcomes for anyone who ventures into the streets and falls into drug addiction: jail, institutions, and death. Throughout my lifetime, I witnessed the carnage that addiction wreaked on our society. My own experiences with incarceration, institutionalization, and near-death events led me to realize that a truly successful drug user simply does not exist.

Drug and alcohol addiction claimed the lives of many family members, friends, and close associates. In my family of seven siblings, three died directly from drug use, while three others indulged in alcohol and other illicit substances. Today, only my oldest brother and I survive from that generation. Even my aunts and uncles were ensnared by drugs or alcohol, rendering their lives unmanageable. I consider myself blessed to have broken the generational curse of rampant addiction and thank God that my children have grown up drug-free.

The first casualty in our family was my brother Marvin. He was an intelligent man who attended Morgan State University and was a talented tailor. Later, he became a

Baltimore City firefighter and eventually ventured into the drug game, working as a lieutenant for my other brother, Clarence. Initially, Marvin operated in the drug trade without succumbing to mind-altering substances. However, amid the high-paced street life and the burden of managing a legion of young dealers, he succumbed to the temptations of drug use. At first, he seemed to function well—maintaining his job and providing for his family—but eventually, the disease of addiction took complete control. On June 6, 1992, Marvin was found dead in his home from an apparent drug overdose. Although it was common knowledge among some of us that he had been using drugs, his wife and children were likely shielded from the truth, and his exact cause of death was never disclosed.

Unlike notorious drug dealers like Peanut King, Junior Bunk, and Little Melvin, my brother Clarence managed to remain one of Baltimore City's most elusive drug dealers. He had an uncanny ability to stay under the radar—he never wore flashy clothes, drove an expensive car, and kept his inner circle tight. He operated his organization discreetly, with Marvin playing a major role behind the scenes.

Occasionally, Clarence would host private parties for his closest friends, and I was invited to attend. I was deeply involved in street life at the time, using heroin daily. Clarence was cautious around me, aware that my behavior was unpredictable; I would seize every opportunity to feed my addiction, though I never contemplated robbing my own brother. I remember attending one such party where a smorgasbord of drugs was displayed—heroin, cocaine, marijuana, hallucinogens like windowpane and microdot, and an array of other illicit substances. That sight made me realize that heroin was just one part of his drug distribution operation.

At these parties, which typically hosted fifteen to twenty people, some danced to loud music, others indulged in drugs, and still others engaged in casual conversation. Clarence would quietly observe from a distance, wearing dark sunglasses. He rarely engaged in conversation, but when he did speak, everyone listened. Despite his reputation in the drug world, he was a health nut who didn't indulge in drugs at the parties. The gatherings would often last until the next morning, with those too inebriated finding a place to crash in the apartment.

Later, Clarence partnered with a man from New York to establish legitimate businesses—a taxicab company, a couple of laundromats, and he owned at least three houses. However, a woman he had entrusted to run one of his stash houses was arrested with a large quantity of drugs, and surveillance evidence linked Clarence to the operation. He went to trial and was convicted of manufacturing and distributing narcotics. The government seized all his personal assets, and his New York partner took over the businesses.

After serving approximately nine years, Clarence was released. Before his incarceration, he had managed to stash a large sum of money. Upon his release, he moved in with a lady friend and took a job at the House of Pancakes as a cook. Unable to reconcile with the loss of all he had accomplished, Clarence eventually returned to drug use. His health deteriorated—he was diagnosed with emphysema, which worsened as he continued to use drugs. His savings dwindled, and he lived paycheck to paycheck. On March 24, 1998, Clarence was found dead on his living room floor from a drug overdose, discovered by his live-in girlfriend.

Writing about my sister Carolyn is challenging because she kept most of her activities private. I suspect she had an active sex life, though I never saw her with any partner—male or female. I cannot say for certain whether she was straight, gay, or bisexual, but I do know she loved to get high and party, indulging in whatever drugs were available. Her plus-size figure, compounded by an unhealthy eating regimen, put her at high risk for health problems. She was a fun-loving person who enjoyed watching the neighborhood children. Carolyn never seemed to hold a traditional 9-to-5 job; instead, she always resided with our older sister Patsy and babysat for families in the community.

Due to her unhealthy lifestyle, Carolyn was diagnosed with a chronic physical illness that resulted in a brief hospitalization. After her release, she was prescribed narcotics to manage her symptoms. I vividly remember visiting her one day when it was evident that she was under the influence of heavy sedatives. Her appearance filled me with deep sorrow; as someone in recovery, seeing her in that condition was a stark reminder of the devastating consequences of drug addiction.

On March 11, 2013, while I was working, I received a call from my niece Tonya asking me to visit her mother's house. When I arrived, I was given the devastating news that my sister Carolyn had passed away in her sleep. Paramedics arrived about five minutes later, and upon entering her bedroom, they noted that rigor mortis had already set in. Carolyn was pronounced deceased, and the funeral home was called to retrieve her body. It was later determined that she had died from being over-medicated with the prescribed drugs given to her upon her release.

My sister Patsy was the glue that held our family together. In her early twenties, she took on the monumental responsibility of caring for Carolyn and me after our mother's death. Even though she had two young daughters of her own, she was the sole reason my sister and I avoided foster care. Raising a teenage heroin addict was daunting, but Patsy never gave up on me. She had two distinct personalities: one, a stern woman who accepted no nonsense from anyone; and the other, a kind-hearted soul who cared for anyone in need. She even raised foster children until they became adults.

Like our mother, Patsy was obsessed with keeping a clean house—her home was always immaculate, despite her limited literacy. Though our family was steeped in alcohol and drug abuse, Patsy maintained her job, paid her bills, and raised two wonderful daughters. She enjoyed smoking marijuana, drinking alcohol, and hosting family gatherings on most weekends and holidays.

Patsy, however, suffered from back pain and high blood pressure—a condition common in our family. Her doctor attributed these issues to her weight, though she was not obese but simply plus-size. Eventually, her doctor referred her to a bariatric physician who convinced her to undergo gastric bypass surgery. Patsy consulted with my brother's girlfriend, Lydia, who had lost a significant amount of weight after her surgery, and she decided to follow suit. Unfortunately, the surgery turned out to be the worst decision of her life. A couple of months later, Patsy developed chronic kidney failure and had to undergo dialysis treatment. Her weight dwindled to 105 pounds as she continued fighting for her life, spending months in and out of nursing homes until she was finally admitted to Johns Hopkins Hospital in intensive care.

On December 20, 2016, I remember a social worker from Johns Hopkins calling family members to the hospital because Patsy had taken a turn for the worse. I was working when my niece called me to come over. When I arrived, family and friends gathered around Patsy in prayer. Only immediate family was allowed in her room, so I waited in the family room while my two nieces stayed with her. One of my nieces even climbed into her bed with Patsy and held her until she passed.

My brother Larry and I were the closest among our siblings, sharing a room and playing sports together during our younger years. Larry was intelligent and studious, and people believed he was destined for success. Yet, as time passed, I saw a change in him. I believed his tortured soul and deeply buried trauma began to emerge. His comedic persona became a smokescreen to hide his inner pain. Although three of my brothers were known to be children of Jerome Fowlkes, Larry did not resemble them, leading his father to deny his paternity—a denial that affected him in unimaginable ways. I wonder if that rejection contributed to the drastic changes in his personality and ambitions.

In retrospect, Larry's behavior grew increasingly abnormal. He deliberately hurt or killed animals—hitting dogs with his car, swinging cats by their tails, and throwing them high into the air. When punished with an extension cord for his unruly behavior, he would grit his teeth and endure the lashings without shedding a tear. He was quick to fight, and I never saw him lose. Despite his aggressive behavior, people were drawn to his humor and comedic antics.

Larry eventually began using heroin later in life, and despite being fun to hang out with, he developed a reputation for being dangerous—if you crossed him, he would come after you. I had no idea he was using until one day he approached me about making money. I was still active in my addiction, and he mentioned a small-time drug dealer he wanted to rob. I couldn't get a real gun, so I managed to procure a fake replica of a 9mm pistol. We drove to the dealer's home; I knocked on the door, and when a man answered, I drew my replica and demanded his money and drugs. When he resisted, I struck him on the head with the fake gun, which broke in half as I clutched it together, and I collected a small amount of money and drugs. After that heist with Larry, I felt ashamed—not because I had robbed someone, but because I had allowed my brother to see me in that light. I never again participated in any criminal activities with him.

On September 25, 2017, nearly a year after the death of our sister Patsy, I received a call from Larry's daughter asking me to come to their home. When I arrived, I noticed the somber expressions on the faces of my niece and her mother. Larry's fiancé explained that she and her daughter had gone to buy groceries, and when they returned, they found Larry's lifeless body lying on the bedroom floor. Ironically, Larry had predicted his own death. I remembered giving him a ride home from Patsy's funeral, and he had remarked that he was next. Although I was annoyed by his comment, having already lost four siblings, his words spoke volumes about the torment in his soul. Nearly a year later, Larry died alone in his bedroom from a drug overdose.

I cannot emphasize enough how grateful I am that God granted me the strength to break the generational curse of rampant addiction that had plagued our family for generations. I am equally thankful for the opportunity to have been a part of my family members' lives. Each one is forever ingrained in my spirit and memory. My oldest brother Syvester, for example, underwent a liver transplant after years of chronic drinking; he and I are the only surviving members of our immediate family. Today, Syvester is alcohol-free, and we share a loving relationship.

CHAPTER FORTY-FIVE
The Lessons of Death

I have witnessed a great deal of death in my lifetime, and with each loss, I've come to understand that every person who crossed my path played a significant role in shaping who I am today. My mother, who graced my life for sixteen years, left an indelible mark on me. Although her death was a deep trauma that instilled in me a lifelong fear of abandonment by those who claim to love me, I have come to realize that my desperate need for her presence skewed my understanding of her passing. My self-centeredness made her death about my loss rather than acknowledging it as a natural, necessary evolution of her life's purpose. Over time, I have come to believe that death is not an end, but rather the spirit's journey through this universe.

The deaths of my siblings, relatives, friends, and fellow Narcotics Anonymous members have each served a unique purpose in my life. These losses have given me a broader perspective on mortality, reminding me that we are all born only to eventually die. Death has taught me to live each day as if it were my last—to seek happiness and fulfillment in every moment. I have been on a long journey of self-discovery and change, and with every new experience, I realize that I have only scratched the surface of transforming my belief systems. I strive to become untethered from the inner and outer disturbances—fear, insecurity, and feelings of inadequacy—that have held me captive for so long.

I have learned that in order to live freely, I must understand that my inner thoughts do not define me. I cannot validate or give credence to the negative voices that whisper doubts about myself and others. Silencing these inner demons is not easy, but it is essential to my continued growth.

As I close this chapter and this book, I carry with me the hard-won lessons of death and loss. I honor every life that has touched mine, knowing that each departure has propelled me further on my journey toward healing. In embracing the inevitability of death, I have learned to cherish life more deeply, to seek beauty in every fleeting moment, and to remain ever committed to the pursuit of self-love and transformation.

About the Author

Donald M. Smith, MSW, LMSW, is a dedicated advocate, educator, and survivor whose life journey serves as a vivid testament to perseverance and hope. Born and raised in the tumultuous neighborhoods of Baltimore, Donald experienced firsthand the harsh realities of systemic inequality, economic hardship, and social injustice.

Amid these challenges, he became intimately acquainted with the struggles of addiction, witnessing both its destructive force within his community and its impact on his own life. Rather than succumbing to despair, however, Donald chose to forge a path marked by healing, growth, and an unwavering commitment to helping others break free from cycles of trauma and addiction.

Donald's pursuit of higher education began as a personal quest for transformation. Determined to understand the complexities of human behavior and the root causes of substance abuse, he embarked on a journey toward earning a Master's degree in Social Work. This academic achievement, combined with his professional designation as a Licensed Master Social Worker (LMSW), reflects his deep-rooted desire to serve individuals and families who, like himself, have grappled with life's toughest obstacles. Whether providing one-on-one counseling or facilitating group therapy sessions, Donald emphasizes empathy, cultural competence, and evidence-based practices, always striving to meet people where they are in their recovery process.

Donald's memoir stands as both a cautionary tale and a source of inspiration. Through candid storytelling, he offers an honest look at the depths of substance abuse, illustrating how adverse circumstances can lead even the most hopeful among us astray. Yet his narrative also serves as a beacon of possibility, underscoring that redemption, while never simple, remains within reach for those committed to reclaiming their lives. In all that he does—be it writing, volunteering, or mentoring—Donald endeavors to uplift others with a message that healing and restoration are achievable goals, and that one person's story has the power to inspire a collective awakening.

Donald Smith brings years of experience to his role as a skilled wood craftsman as the sole proprietor of Trailer Countertop and Cabinet Design, LLC. Over the years, he has finely honed his carpentry skills, allowing him to offer a wealth of expertise in creating custom solutions for his clients. To explore Donald's work or inquire about services, visit his business website at www.mobiletrailerdesign.com.

www.ingramcontent.com/pod-product-compliance
Lightning Source LLC
Chambersburg PA
CBHW021616120626
46545CB00001B/262